50 Ugly Faces Of Immorality Exposed

50 evil effects and 28 ways out of the bondage
(An Encyclopaedic Approach)

For Youths and Adults
Married and Unmarried
For the Purpose of Holiness
Within and Without

Pastor Izuora Annacletus Obiora

ISBN: 978-1-9996642-8-2

DEDICATION

This Book is dedicated to God the father, God the son, God the Holy Spirit.

To my beloved wife, Ify Comfort Izuora, my children, Godson and Divine Favour Izuora, and to all my extended family who are courageous enough to be born again.

To all the Christian soldiers, members of the Army of the Lord who overcame the Jezebels and the Delilahs, and all the powers of immorality.

To all the Ministers, the Elders, the workers and the members of the Mountain of Fire and Miracles Ministries, Senegal

Finally, to my beloved mother Late Mrs. Magdaleine Izuora.

ACKNOWLEDGEMENT

I use this opportunity to thank our Father in the Lord.

Dr. D.K. Olukoya whose ministration made me to realise who I am, that was in April 1999.

Under this four-star general of the Lord, I got my training as a soldier of Christ, he is the general overseer of Mountain of fire and Miracles Ministries worldwide. Next is my beautiful and lovely wife whose ceaseless prayer made this divine dream to manifest.

Next is, mummy Augusta Ijeoma Onyemuche, an amazon of the Lord, who carried me on her shoulder until I was able to stand on my own feet. I will not forget my brother Chief O.C Ibekwe CEO Osibisa Global link PLC Eze Chukwukwadolu 1 na Ozoubulu and his beautiful wife, who has helped me to move forward in many ways, thank you my brother, your effort to make my work easy is highly appreciated. Chief Fortune Obasi Uburu ka nkwu 1 na Enugu state and his wife who have also contributed in their own way to help in this book becoming a reality. To all the Ministers, the Pastor, the Elders, the workers, and the members of M.F.M. Senegal, I thank you for your cooperation with me in my Ministry. Sister Yinka, God bless you for your tremendous support. My son, Festy, God bless you. Sister Juliet Enaluna Omorighe thanks so much and my son Emmanuel Ricks, I appreciate you much. Tony Okugbo, Tony Emechata, Tony nwokolo, Favour Ugwu, and many more I appreciate you all. Sister Ann Koroma has worked tirelessly in typing all the manuscript and those of the other books I have written. I pray therefore that God Almighty will bless you all and answer your prayers in Jesus' name.

Chaplain sub–LT Comm Izuora Annacletus.O. B A. HONS Eng /Lit Uniben.

TABLE OF CONTENTS

Dedication iii

Acknowledgement v

Preface ix

Be Born Again x

Chapter One
Introduction: Immorality The Deadliest Sin 1

Chapter Two
Some Wrong Notions About Sexual Immorality 11

Chapter Three
Fifty Ugly Faces Of Immorality 23

Chapter Four
Causes Of Sexual Immorality 51

Chapter Five
Effects Of Sexual Immorality 67

Chapter Six
28 Ways Out Of The Bondage Of Immorality 87

Chapter Seven
Run For Your Dear Life 97

Other Books By The Same Author 102

Bibliography 105

PREFACE

The purpose of this work is to expose the many faces of immorality, their evil effects and the ways out. Here, the wrong notions people have for committing immorality have been weighed, tried and found wanting, and all the powers and principalities that are behind sexual immorality are exposed including their evil works and activities.

The major aim of this work is to warn the children of God that are still in the bandwagon of the world, the children of God who are still with the multitude, those who are still in the bus of immorality whose destination is hellfire, for them to jump out before it becomes too late.

Again, the work is for every group of Christians, the youth and the adult, the spinsters and the bachelors for the purpose of holiness within and without. Also, for holiness and righteousness to reign in the church of Christ. The Jezebels and the Delilahs are working round the clock to fulfil their evil assignments. Ministers of God should better beware so that they are not pulled down. That their individual ministries are not terminated. Every minister has his own Bathsheba. Every Samson has his own Delilah, and every prophet of God has his own Jezebel. You had better be empowered to overcome these Jezebels, Bathsheba's and Delilahs so that they will not shave your hair and destroy your ministry.

BE BORN AGAIN

Oh, have you not heard
That Jesus for you died.
Or have you not seen God?
On the cross his hands
Outspread to receive mankind?
Why- - - - - - -?

What? What is it you wait for?
Have you not heard?
The messianic message
The message of salvation
The message of the kingdom
Now

That way go you not anymore.
To our redeemer the lamb turn
This concept let us all accept.
Once there is life after death
Man must live God's kind of life on Earth.

Izuora Cley. O. UniBen January 1, 1990

CHAPTER ONE

~

Introduction: Immorality
The Deadliest Sin

"For the commandment is a lamp and the law is light and reproof of instructions are the ways of life. To keep thee from the evil woman from the flatery of the tongue of a strange woman. Lust not after her beauty in thine heart neither let her take thee with her eyelids.

For by means of whorish woman a man is brought to piece of bread and the adultress will hunt for the precious life. Can a man take fire in his bossom and his clothes not be burned?

Can one go upon hot coals and his feet not be burned? So, he that goeth in to his neighbours wife whosoever toucheth her shall not be innocent.

But whose committeth adultery with a woman lacketh understanding he that doeseth it destroyeth his own soul. A wound and dishonour shall he get and his reproach shall not be wiped away for jealousy is the rage of a man. Therefore he will not spare in the day of vengence. He will not regard any ransom. Neither will he rest content though thou givest many gifts." Proverbs 6:23-35

S exual immorality is the most rampant and most deadly sin in the whole world. In fact, it breeds other sins like lying, murder, stealing abortion, worldliness, craze for fashion, love of money, covetousness and so on.

Sexual immorality is a sin that opens door to the enemy and gives witchcraft powers, dream criminals and the evil powers of one's father's house the legal ground to attack.

Through sexual immorality, many have fragmented their lives, blocked their blessings, grieved and quenched the fire of the Holy Spirit, diverted their destinies, buried their potentials and virtues, killed their calling and their ministries and given their enemies such as household wickedness, marine powers, and ancestral and familiar spirits weapons to attack them.

Many have also opened the door to spirit wife and spirit husband into their lives and brought in poverty, lack, want and wretchedness into their lives. Sexual immorality is a sin that has many other sins on queue behind it. Once you indulge in it you see yourself indulging in others automatically.

Many have contacted venereal diseases, curable and incurable. Many have even died because of this sin.

Sexual immorality is a sin that kills a man in the time his life is at its sweetest to him. The Bible says that the way of a sinner is hard. God hates this sin so much that He took time to explain laws guiding man and women relationship. Because of sexual immorality Sodom and Gomorrah were destroyed with fire and only Lot and his daughters were saved.

On account of sexual immorality the two daughters of Lot had two sons, Moab and Ammon by their father Lot. They came out of Sodom, but Sodom refused to come out of them. Because of sexual immorality, Reuben the first son of Jacob lost his position as the first son in the heart of his father and was replaced by Ephraim the second son of Joseph. What did Reuben do? He slept with one of his father's wives and instead of a blessing he received a curse from his father while others were blessed.

> *"Reuben Thou art my first born, my might and the Beginning of my strength, the excellence of dignity And the Excellency of power. Unstable as water, Thou shall not excel because thou wentest up to thy Father's bed then defiledst thou it, he went up to my couch" Genesis 49: 3-4*

Owing to sexual immorality, Samson the strongest man who ever lived since the world was created, lost the Holy Spirit, lost the glory of God in his life, his hair, the symbol of his glory, power and anointing, was shaved by Delilah and Samson the strongest man became a plaything, a mere toy in the hands of his enemies. Through sexual immorality, David a man after God's heart grieved God. He coveted another man's wife Bathsheba and murdered Uriah the husband, but his case was somehow different because he repented immediately and made amends, but immorality, murder, confusion and war became the order of the day in his household. Ammon his son raped his half-sister, Tamma by the same father, David.

Absalom his son, slept with his (David) wives in the open upon the housetop where all Israel saw them. Absalom murdered Ammon because Tamar and Absalom came from the same mother. Finally, Absalom planned a coup d'état to overthrow his father David and launched attack and pursued his father out of his land.

All these because of one single offence of adultery. How much more will those swimming in it suffers the consequences? Through sexual immorality, many Generals of the Lord have been demoted to mere recruits, servants, gatemen and gardeners while some were totally removed.

Apostle Paul warned us when he said.

> "Wherefore let him that thinketh He standeth. Take heed lest he falls" 1 Corinthians 10:2.

Solomon, the wisest king who had ever lived, had seven hundred wives and three hundred concubines a total of one thousand women. Of course, through love of pleasure of women he went into idolatry in order to please his wives thereby displeasing God.

The wisest king became the most foolish person. To marry more than one wife is foolishness enough, an error that can never be mended once the strange woman, the second, third or fourth wife has children, how much more one thousand women. It was a license unto those women for sexual immorality and sexual perversion, such as lesbianism, masturbation, prostitution, adultery and so on. He offended God through polygamy and idolatry. Through sexual immorality many men have been murdered and their wives taken. Many girls have died in the process of abortion and many unwanted children, bastards have been born.

Through sexual immorality, many agents of Satan have hooked and destroyed the ministries of many men of God. Sexual immorality is the major work of the flesh and others follow it.

Paul in Galatians 5:19 says

"Now the works of the flesh are manifest Which are these Adultery, fornication Uncleanness, lasciviousness...."

The first four works of the flesh fall under immorality before others began to follow. Sexual immorality is a sin that keeps people in bondage. Once you go into it, you are hooked, you will like to go again, the more you indulge in it the deeper you go, the more you desire it. No fornicator or adulterer can be satisfied even if he indulges in its daily.

Sex cannot satisfy the desire for it until you crucify the flesh and the lust thereof, until you are delivered from the powers of immorality you will continue to indulge in it. even when you do not want to do it, you will still see yourself doing it.

An immoral man or woman has no class. He or she can do it with an old person or with an under aged person. They also have no choice or taste. They can lust after and sleep with any person, sick or health a prostitute or not, a mad person or a sane person, dirty or neat person, a housemaid or even his or her relative.

They have a drive, a fore, a demon pushing them when the fever comes upon them, no more sleep, no more rest until they commit immorality.

It is like drug addiction, when they satisfy their desire for that moment, the next moment the desire surges up again especially when the thought comes into their heart or when they see somebody they like.

God made us and called us to be holy. He hates immorality with perfect hatred and do not relate or fellowship with immoral, unclean, defiled, and polluted people. Our body is the temple of the Holy Spirit and they Holy Spirit does not stay in any house that is dirty and smelly.

Paul in 1 Corinthians 3:16-17 states...

> *"Know you not that you are the temple of God that the spirit of God dwelleth in you? if any man defiles the temple of God him shall God destroy, for the temple of God is holy which temple ye are"*

The commonest way of defiling the temple of God is through immorality. The commonest way of grieving the Holy Spirit of God which dwelleth in you is through immorality. The commonest way of opening doors for the enemy to enter and attack one is through immorality. The commonest way to entering satanic bondages is through immorality. The commonest way of provoking God to anger is through immorality. The easiest and quickest way of backsliding is through immorality.

Immorality can bring curses into one's life and at the same time it strengthens old evil covenants. It is the easiest way of making one to have a closed heaven, a heaven of brass and the persons earth, will become iron.

Immorality blocks Gods ears to our prayers and closes His eyes and turns away His face from our suffering. God hates immorality with perfect hatred.

Paul in 1 Corinthians 6:13b-20 states...

> *"Now the body is not for fornication but for the Lord and the Lord for the body know ye not that your bodies are the members of Christ? Shall I then take members of Christ and make them the members of a harlot? God forbid what? know ye not that he which is joined to an harlot is one body? for two, saith he shall be one flesh.*
>
> *But he that is joined unto the Lord is one spirit. Flee fornication. Every sin that a man doeth is without the body but he that committeth fornication sinneth against his own body. What?*
>
> *know ye not your body is the temple of the Holy Ghost which is in you, which you have of God and ye are not your own? For you are bought with a price therefore glory God in your body and in your spirit, which are Gods."*

The message is to the children of God. Many children of God are operating under the bondage of immorality and they need urgent help in form of deliverance. There are agents of immorality in the houses of God today. One day, a lady came to a pastor for counselling and told the pastor that if any man asked her for sex that she had not refused. she was telling the pastor that if he was interested that she was ready. She was an agent, but she failed in that assignment.

There are many children of God that have forsaken their first love, denied God, betrayed Jesus and crucified Him afresh and have embraced and loved the world and its lusts thereby making themselves enemies of God.

Sexual immorality is the major ministerial pitfall awaiting the ministers of God at every corner, it is the most powerful tool in the hand of Satan. It is also the commonest and the deadliest. Once a child of God indulges in it, his or her dance steps will change immediately, and the person will get back to "zero level". if the grace is abundant in the person's life, he or she will start over again and all the former works the person has done will no more be remembered. If the grace is not sufficient in the life of the person, he or she will fall out of the presence of God and the devil will thoroughly deal with the person.

In the house of God today, we have the Delilah's and the Jezebel whose main assignment is to pull down the men of God and destroy their respective ministries. In the book of Judges 16v18-20 we see how Delilah destroyed Samson and terminated his ministry.

The book of Revelation 2:20-23 also says

> *"Notwithstanding, I have a few things against thee because thou sufferest that woman Jezebel which calleth herself a prophetess, to teach and to seduce my servants to commit fornication and to eat things sacrificed to idols*
>
> *And I gave her space to repent of her fornication and she repented not. Behold, I will cast her into a bed and them that commit adultery with her into great tribulation except they repent of*

their deeds. And I will kill her children with death and all the Churches shall know that I am he which searches the reins and hearts and I will give unto every one of you according to your work"

The warning is not to unbelievers. It was originally to the children of God in Thyatira then but now to all children of God everywhere. The Jezebel of Thyatira specialises in seducing and teaching the men of God to commit sexual immorality. Jezebel of this type are in every Church. God gave her space to repent but she refused to repent which shows that she is an agent, and she knew very well what she was doing, and this same woman was known as a prophetess which will automatically bring other servants of God close to her who ignorantly will walk into her " lap trap" she was a wolf in sheep's clothing.

Punishment is awaiting every adulterer, every fornicator that refuses to repent. God shall destroy everyone that defile the temple of God. He shall bring great tribulation upon the immoral people and their bastard children shall partake in the suffering. The only way out of this pending punishment is REPENTANCE!

PRAYER POINTS

Pray these prayers with holy violence and anger

1. Every seed of sexual immorality in my life, roast by fire in Jesus' name

2. Every arrow of sexual immorality fired into my life, come out and die in Jesus' name

3. You lust of the eyes in my life die by fire in Jesus' name

4. I shall not be trapped into immorality in Jesus' name

5. You evil powers of my father's house pushing me into immorality, release me and die in Jesus' name

6. You witchcraft spell of immorality, die in Jesus' name

7. Thou power of sexual immorality, break and die in Jesus' name

8. Every pitfall of immorality on my way, be covered by the blood of Jesus

9. Every Delilah targeting my ministry, die in Jesus' name

10. You marine powers planning against my ministry, fail woefully

11. Every witchcraft network against my destiny, scatter by fire

12. You destiny diverters, release my destiny and die in Jesus' name

13. You star hunters, release my star and die in Jesus' name

CHAPTER TWO

—— ∽ ——

Some Wrong Notions About Sexual Immorality

"There is a way which seemeth right Unto a man but the end thereof are. The ways of death" Proverbs 14:12

A lot of people who have decided to perish instead of repenting and forsaking their immoral ways have devised a lot of excuses for committing sexual immorality. There are some notions, some concepts not well founded, beliefs upon which the paraphiliacs anchor to commit sexual immorality. But these groups of people are making serious mistakes. When they die, during judgement time, they will discover, when they cannot right their wrongs, that God does not accept any excuse for committing sin.

The Bible says that there is a way which seemeth right unto a man, but the end thereof are the ways of death. So, it will be with all that are swimming and wallowing in the quagmire of sexual immorality. Unless they repent and receive Jesus Christ and reject every lust of the eyes and the flesh and crucify and mortify and put their flesh under and begin to walk in the spirit, they will all cry "had I known."

Among the so many wrong notions about sexual immorality are:

1. THAT MARRIAGE IS IMMUNITY AGAINST SEXUAL IMMORALILTY

People who get caught in the net of paraphilia always justify themselves that they do it because they are not yet married. They say that when they get married. They go in and mind their spouses and will no longer indulge in fornication. But that belief they have is a mere wishful thinking because such people when they marry will graduate from fornication into adultery. They will be unfaithful to their spouses because what makes them immoral is inside them. Once it rears its ugly head, they lust and go ahead to commit adultery.

2. THAT THE DESIRE FOR SEXUAL IMMORALITY CAN BE SUPPRESSED

Some people believe that they are strong, righteous and holy enough to suppress evil sexual desire and abstain from it. The suppression of the desire can work for a noticeably short period. This period is a period of inconvenience. Once they are in the right place, at the right time in a convenient place alone with the "right" person, whatever sexual desire they have been suppressing will burst open and they will see themselves committing sexual immorality. So, marriage is not immunity neither can the evil desire be suppressed.

3. THAT ONCE NOBODY SEES ME, I AM FREE

Some others parade themselves as holy and righteous children of God, but they are white sepulchres. They are very clever in committing immorality because they believe that, once they are not seen, they are free. They have his commandment which they do obey. Thou shall not be found out. They believe that once it is known it is a sin but if you are clever enough to cover your tracks, there is no problem. This group of people forgets that there is a person that is omnipresent and omniscient, and that person is God. God is watching and He sees and knows everything that is happening.

One sister was cornered by one man and the man thought that he had gotten another meat for his evil pleasure. So, he locked the door and the windows and drew the curtain blinds and turned to the sister, but the sister was still in her dress. He asked the sister what she was waiting for. The sister replied that she was waiting for him to close heaven so that God would not see them, that once he was able to close the eyes of God, she would comply but if he were not able to close the eyes of God, she would not cooperate.

Job. 34:21 says:

"For His eyes are upon the ways of man He seeth all his goings"

4. THAT LONG ABSTINENCE CAUSES ILL HEALTH

Those who believe that long abstinence from sexual intercourse causes one problem or the other in their body. This is not true. A young man that is a virgin will always have a discharge during his sleep when the sperm sac is filled up

Abstinence from sex does not cause boil nor pimple nor any other sickness. Nature controls it.

5. THAT BODY NO BE FIREWOOD OR MAN NO BE WOOD

Some others justify their immoral behaviours by believing and saying that their body "no be firewood" This is because they are still alive to sin. They are not yet dead to sin. The flesh is too much in control of their lives. They have not put their flesh under where it is supposed to be. They enthroned the flesh, and they glorify it, so when the flesh desired evil they give in to it saying that "body no be firewood"

6. THAT A FISH IN THE WATER CANNOT DENY WATER AND ANY MAN ON EARTH CANNOT DENY SIN

These categories of people argue that no one can be holy because every person in the world is like fish in the water that cannot deny water and anyone on earth cannot deny sin. This view is not true because though we are in the world, we are born gain children of God we are not of the world. If the fish in the water cannot deny water, it is because it still alive in water and to water. What of the fish that had been caught by the fishermen out of the water and is dried-up very well by fire? This fish cannot it deny water? Some people put up this defence because they have not yet been caught and dried up in the fire of Holy Ghost. When the fire of God will come upon them, they will dry up and still be in the world without sin and moreover. God called us unto holiness and not unto immorality.

Jesus says in Matthew 5:48

"Be ye therefore perfect even as your father. Which is in heaven is perfect"

7. THAT I WILL ASK FOR FORGIVENESS AFTER

Several people when they are caught in the fever of immorality, they will encourage themselves by believing that they will ask for forgiveness after. But the Bible calls this type of sin wilful sin. You know that it is wrong, and you still went ahead and did its God forgives sins committed inadvertently but for advertently committed sin, the person will bear the punishment.

8. THAT LOOKING IS FREE

Some people believe that looking is free. We were thought in the School of deliverance that the first look is normal, but the second look is a sin, and the Bible calls it the lust of the eyes which leads to evil desires. An adage says that what the eyes do not see, the heart does not desire.

Jesus when he was teaching about adultery says:

> *"But I say unto you that whosoever. Looketh on a woman to lust after. Her has committed adultery with. Her already in his heart."* Mathew 5:28

Jesus went ahead in verse 29 of the same chapter to advise us.

> *"If thy right eye offends thee pluck it out. And cast it from thee for it is profitable. For thee that one of thy members should. Perish and not that thy whole body should be cast into hell".*

In Matthew 6:22-23 Jesus tells us...

> *"The light of the body is the eye, If therefore thine eye be single. Thy whole body shall be full of light. But if thine eye be evil, thy*

whole body Shall be full of darkness. If therefore the Light that is in thee be darkness, how great is that darkness"!

Therefore, looking is not free

- ◆ Looking the second time is sin
- ◆ Looking brings the lust of eyes
- ◆ Looking brings evil desire
- ◆ Looking at evil causes darkness in one's life
- ◆ Looking can take one into hell fire
- ◆ Looking brings evil arrows into one's heart

Job says:

> *"I made a covenant with mine EYES. Why then should I THINK upon a maid?"*

Two words are important to us here, "eyes" and "think" Remember you look with your eyes and think in your heart, so without looking there will be no thinking of any evil in your heart.

Let us see what Jeremiah says in the book of Lamentations 3:51

> *"My EYE affecteth mine HEART because of all the daughters of my city"*

Jeremiah was busy looking at the daughters of his city and the next was that he received an evil arrow and he cried that his eyes had afflicted his heart because he was busy looking at the daughters of his city. Remember that Jeremiah was a young man and he prevailed over the daughters of his own city.

In the case of Isaiah, he cried because the spoiling, the waywardness, the whoredom and the harlotry of the daughters of his people. Hear him in Isaiah 22:4

> *"Therefore, said I, look away from me I will weep bitterly labor not to comfort Me because of the spoiling of the Daughters of my people"*

9. THAT YOU ARE HOLY WHEN YOU DON'T DO IT PHYSICALLY

Some believe that they are holy because physically they do not indulge in sexual immorality. However, they do it in their hearts and in their dreams. Some do not have boyfriends and girlfriends because they have been mandated by their spiritual spouses never to have. So, this group believes that because they do not commit immorality with anybody, they are holy whereas, at night their spiritual husbands and wives will come and defile them. Holiness starts from within.

Apostle Paul in his first letter to the Thessalonians 5:23 prayed for them thus:

> *"And the very God of peace sanctify you Wholly and I pray God your whole SPIRIT And SOUL and BODY be preserved Blameless unto the coming of our Lord Jesus Christ"*

Therefore, if you do not do it physically but you do it with s a spirit wife or husband in your dream, your spirit man is being polluted. In some cases of spirit husband or spirit wife attack, physical evidence are noticed like carrying the man down from the bed, like seeing some money under the pillow when the woman wakes up in the morning or under wear for the lady or physical male semen on the laps of the lady. Other evidence include no physical marriage, late marriage, no children for the earthly husband and so on.

Consequently, when you call yourself a child of God, you must keep away from sin of immorality, spirit husband or wife must die, and you will be free from his/her bondage before you begin to experience true holiness.

10. MY LIFE IS MY OWN I MUST LIVE IT THE WAY I LIKE

This is not true of the children of God. We do not own our lives; we belong to somebody. God, who created us and still bought us with the blood of Jesus. And the Bible made it clear that our body is the temple of God and whosoever will defile it God will destroy.

God created us we belong to Him. Satan separated us from God through sin and God bought us back to himself with the blood of Jesus. Therefore, we doubly belong to Him. Your life is not yours. Whatsoever we do with our bodies, the Lord will judge and reward us accordingly. If you sow in the flesh you will reap corruption and death, if you sow in the spirit, you will reap eternal life.

11. THAT SHE IS MY WIFE THEREFOERE I CANNOT COMMIT SEXUAL IMMORALITY WITH HER

This is also wrong belief. There is what the English man calls paraphilia. This is sexual perversion. When you begin to play with your wife or husband perversely. it is immorality. Examples are: Anal intercourse which is sodomy or oral sex which is known as cunnilingus or going to sleep with your wife when she is undergoing her menstruation. This defiles a man and sodomy, and oral sex are all forms of sexual perversion. Although it is with your spouse, it is immorality before God.

12. THAT I AM STRONG, POWERFUL, HOLY AND WISE; THEREFORE, I CANNOT COMMIT IMMORALITY.

This is a wrong notion because you cannot be stronger and more powerful than Samson who ended up his ministry on the lap of Delilah, and you cannot be holier than David who was a man after God's heart, but he killed Uriah and took Bathsheba. Neither can you be wiser than Solomon who ended up in idolatry through too much of the pleasures of women. King Solomon's record cannot be broken by anybody, Seven hundred wives and three hundred concubines. That means one thousand women for one man. Wonderful!

We have been advised to be sober, watchful and prayerful because our enemy the fake lion is roaming about looking for whom to devour.

Paul says, *"If you think you stand, be careful lest you fall"*.

The story of a man of God of 65 years whom satanic agents pursued for 17 good years and finally seduced is still being told today. At 65 he fell, went for deliverance and started all over.

13. THAT THERE WAS NO REAL ENTRY. IT WAS ONLY KISSING, CARESSING AND ROMANCE

Some believe that if they have romance without real penetration that it is not sin. But you are finding yourself in such a situation where you are kissing, caressing and romancing is immorality enough to take one to hellfire. If therefore there was no real entry, it is therefore due to either fear of unwanted pregnancy or fear of contacting S.T.D and not the fear of God. It is the suppression of the evil sexual desire. If everything is right the person that has gone through kissing, caressing and romancing will also go through the whole thing.

14. THAT SHE IS MY WIFE TO BE THEREFORE I CAN BE SLEEPING WITH HER NOW

This is a satanic fallacy, absolute falsehood and an immorality concept that people who cannot exercise self-control employ in order to continue in their immorality. It is an invented satanic strategy to keep people in the bondage of sexual immorality.

If you are sincere that she is your wife to be, why not wait for that time to come when your conjugation will be legalized. Many have slept together because they believe they were going to get married but later, they did not get married. In the Christian circle, sex before marriage, that is premarital sex, is forbidden, it is immorality. it is sin.

PRAYER POINTS

1. Any satanic doctrine prepared to lead me into sin, die in Jesus' name

2. Any power in my life that is opposing my Christian life die in Jesus' name

3. Oh Lord, let me die to sin and live unto righteousness in Jesus' name

4. Oh Lord, deliver my eyes from lust in Jesus' name.

5. Thou lust of the flesh, die in Jesus' name

6. Every unfriendly friend that wants to pull me down be removed

7. I dedicate my soul, spirit, and body to our Lord Jesus Christ in Jesus name

8. Spirit of holiness and righteousness, possess my life in Jesus' name

9. Oh Lord, empower me to be sober and wise in Jesus' name

10. Let every over-confidence in my life perish by fire in Jesus' name

11. Thou defiling demons attacking my life, die in Jesus' name

12. Thou polluting spirit wife/husband polluting my spiritual life, lose your hold and die by fire

13. Power to live a holy life fall upon my life in Jesus' name

14. Oh Lord empower me to always do your will.

15. Oh Lord empower me to be watchful and prayerful.

CHAPTER THREE

―――――――― ∾ ――――――――

Fifty Ugly Faces Of Immorality

"For at the window of my house I looked through my casment and beheld among the simple ones, I discerned among the youths. A young man void of understanding, passing through the street near her corner and he went the way to her house in the twililght, in the evening in the black and dark night and behold there met him a woman with the atire of a harlot and subtle of heart she is loud and stubborn. Her feet abide not in her house now is she without now in the streets add lieth in wait at every corner so she caught him and kissed him and with an impudent face said unto him, I have peace offering with me this day have I payed my vows therefore come I forth to meet thee diligently to seek thy face and have found thee I have decked my bed with coverings of tapestry with carved works, with fine linen of egypt. I have perfumed my bed with aloes and cinnamon. Let us take our fill of love until the morning, let us solace ourselves with love for the good man is not at home he is gone a long journey... With her much fair speech she caused him to yield. With the flatering of her lips she forced him. He goeth after her straightway as an ox goeth to the slaughter or as a fool to the correction of stocks till a dart stike through his liver. As a bird hasteth to the snare and knoweth not that it is for his life....Let not thine heart decline to her ways. Go not astray in her paths for she has cast down many:

woudnd yea many strong men have been slain by her. Her house is the way to hell, going down to the chambers of death" Proverbs 7:6-27

S exual immorality has so many ugly faces but here I am presenting only fifty of such ugly faces. This is to help the children of God be on their guard to always detect every subtle move of the enemies, Satan, the world and the flesh.

Sexual immorality is so ugly that the act is never done in the open. Nowadays the earth is another Sodom and Gomorrah, prostitutes line the streets every night. The Earth is going "gaga". The earth is drunk with sin of immorality. The Earth is ripe for the consuming fire of God. One minster said that if God did not judge the Earth with fire, He would apologize to Sodom and Gomorrah.

One religious community is now allowing the homosexuals among them as if it is the normal thing. The abominable the accursed among them who are supposed to be banished, ostracized and cast away from among them are being ordained Bishops. Those who are not qualified to be children of God are being made Bishops to take care of the children of God. Before you know what Satan is planning every member of the religious community has already become a homosexual because of their bishop is a homosexual. Agent of Satan in the house of God.

The overlooked what God said that a man shall not lie with mankind as with womankind

"Thou shall not lie with mankind as with womankind it is abomination"

Sexual immorality is so ugly that Apostle Paul warned that it should not even be mentioned among the children of God. Sexual immorality is so ugly that any time the enemies of God want to provoke God to anger, the commonest and most effective weapon is sexual immorality. This arrow of immorality was fired on the Israelites when Aaron molded the golden calf and they rose to play.

God was also provoked at Pisgah. After Balak and Balaam failed in the attempt to curse the children of Israel they through numerous divinations and sacrifices upon many evils alters released the arrows and spirits of immorality and the children of God started sleeping with strange women of Moab.

Zimri, the son of Salu was foolish enough to bring Gozbi the daughter of Zur a Midianite chief into the tent of the Israelites in the presence of Moses but Phineas the grandson of Aaron took up the challenge and killed both with a spear. Twenty-three thousand Israelites died in this place because of the anger of God that was let loose as a result of sexual immorality. God's anger was pacified because of Phinehas' action.

Today the enemy of God and man is still using this weapon of immorality but in many ways such that if the children of God are not careful, they may be indulging in anyone of them consciously or unconsciously thinking that "God understands" when it comes to sin especially sexual pervasion God does not understand because His pure eyes cannot behold iniquity. He removes His face and blocks His ears because of sin so do not ever live in a fool's paradise because He even removed his face from Jesus when Jesus was loaded with the sins he did not commit, the sins of the whole world on the cross of Calvary.

TYPES OF SEXUALIMMORALITY; PAPRPHILISM

Among the sexual sins are:

1. **FORNICATION:** Chamber's 20th Century dictionary defines it as *"a voluntary sexual intercourse of the unmarried sometimes extended to cases where only one of the pair concerned is unmarried".*

This is defiling one's body. God hates it and warns his children in many places of the scriptures against this but today fornication is the order of the day even in the household of God. Many brothers and sisters are living in sin promising that they will marry each other.

Paul in his letter to the Corinthians said in Chapter 8:13b

"Now the body is not for fornication but For the Lord and the Lord for the body"

In verse 18 he simply commanded us to flee fornication why? It is because

"Every sin that a man doeth is without the Body but he that committeth fornication Sinneth against his own body"

Today they call it "having fun".

2. **ADULTERY:** Chambers 20th Century Dictionary defines it as *"violation of the marriage bed whether one's own or another's"* it is sexual sin between a man and another man's wife or a woman and another woman's husband.

It is unfaithfulness among the married.

Exodus 20:14 God commanded

"Moreover, thou shall not lie carnally with thy neighbors' wife to defile thyself with her"

3. **MASTURBATION:** Chambers Dictionary defines it as *"Stimulation usually by oneself of the sexual organs by manipulation so as to produce orgasm"*. Many things can cause this, such as Sexual thoughts, blue films, pornographic magazines and lack of self-control and so on.

Christians should avoid anything that will bring impure thoughts in their minds. Some that have this masturbation as a habit are in a profoundly serious and strong bondage of immorality. It is only the Lord Jesus Christ that can deliver them.

4. **VOYEURISM:** This is defined as *"One who derives gratification from surreptitiously watching sexual acts or objects"*. This is also called a "PEEPING TOM". There are many kinds of peeping toms. Some move about into the night to peep through the windows of married couples.

Some go to hotels and ask the prostitutes to remove their dresses and they will only look at their body without sleeping with them, they pay them for just looking at them.

This group of people, the actual act does not satisfy them they only take pleasure in looking and they will be satisfied. They really reach orgasm, it is immorality.

5. **PORNOGRAPHIC MAGAZINES:** Some people desire sexual satisfaction by looking at pornographic magazines. Pictures of naked males and females in nude give them pleasure

that they pack quantities of assorted types of these pictures under their beds, pillows or bookcases so that at any time they need them they will be handy. What you watch with your eyes can be the genesis of a lifetime problem.

6. **BLUE FILM:** To some people it is blue movies that give them sexual satisfaction. They have hundreds of them, they watch to corrupt their minds and to defile themselves.

Remember what the eyes do not see the heart does not desire, if what you take in is bad what you will bring out will also be bad "Garbage in Garbage out".

7. **EROTICA:** This refers to erotic literature. There are novels that are dripping with sex. Reading of such novels induces sexual desire.

There are many such novels in the market today. Harold Robins books are in this category. Lolly magazine is also in this group. Christians should avoid reading such dangerous books.

8. **SADO MASOCHISM:** This is defined as "sexual pleasure in being dominated or treated cruelly by the other sex. Morbid gratification in suffering pain, Physical or mental."

This is sexual perversion of a strange kind. For this group of people nothing will turn them on sexual except pain. Something bitter and cruel and for them to reach climax, it is hatred and warfare. A masochist will ask the partner to smack, slap, beat her or him seriously during the sexual acts. Some that are wives are fond of nagging so much which automatically results in their husbands beating them every time. They know what they are doing.

9. **PROSTITUTION:** This is also called SEXPLOITAION, HARLOTRY, WHOREDOM OR MERETRICIOUSNESS (MERETICS). This is the business of hiring oneself out for sexual intercourse in order to receive a pay. In Deuteronomy 23:17 God commanded.

"There shall be no whore of the Daughters of Israel"

But harlotry is the order of the day these days even in the Church there are many Delilahs and Jezebels, that are in the Church for that purpose.

A long time ago prostitution was an evil trade but today men have glorified it. Parents now support their daughters to go into prostitution. Parents collaborate and wangle their teenage daughters into Italy where they prostitute and get abominable money for them. There is a particular state in Nigeria that is known for this.

There are hawkers that hawk their bodies and there are student prostitutes. There are also married prostitutes, but we have the main one that is professional prostitutes.

10. **EXHIBITIONISM:** This is defined as *"Extravagant behaviours aimed at drawing attention to self. Perversion involving public exposure of one's sexual organs"*

This group, the wear miniskirts, body hug, slit skirts, transparent dresses and many other dressers that can expose their breast, the belly or the laps or the tight fitted dresses that can expose the figure as if the person is not putting on anything. This is immorality because they are advertising themselves to the opposite sex. It makes the opposite sex to lust and entertain immoral desires. In extreme cases, it causes rape.

11. **SEDUCTION:** This is to entice somebody to have sexual intercourse with the opposite sex. This can be done through many ways such as body languages, frequent visit, mode of dressing, lavishing of presents upon the person, giving of money, through the eyes or smile or through flattering. it is also called sexual appeal.

Some people have seducing spirit. Every action or movement they make is an invitation for sexual intercourse.

12. **BEASTITIALITY:** This is the act of sleeping with an animal as a human being. Many of our Italian girls have slept with dogs for money. In Zamfara State, a young man appeared before the sharia court for sleeping with pigs. In one of his messages Dr. Olukoya mentioned a man that keeps a duck in his parlour for sexual immorality. Somewhere in western Nigeria a sheep gave birth to a lamb with a human head, but the body was animal's body. There are many examples of how low mankind has degenerated in immorality but God in Leviticus 18:23...

"Neither shall thou lie with any beast to defile thyself therewith, Neither shall any woman stand before a beast to lie down thereunto it is confusion"

13. **UNCLEANNESS:** This is another ugly face of immorality. It is living a life of defilement though sexual immorality. Uncleanness is something impure, defiled, dirty and unholy. One can be unclean through looking, entertaining impure and unwholesome thoughts, touching or even listening and talking. There is what is called ablution, that is, the washing of face, eyes, ears, mouths, hands and feet and even the private parts by the Muslims. In Judaism, they also had such practice

that was why Christ washed the feet of His disciples because they believed that the world is already contaminated and in mingling with the world one becomes unclean hence ablution.

However, Paul in warning the Galatians against the works of the flesh he said

> *"Now the works of the flesh are Made manifest which are these, adultery, fornication, uncleanness lasciviousness..." Galatians 3:19*

The first four are about immorality, uncleanness, being the number three. In his 1st letter to the Thessalonians 4:7 he warned thus

> *"For God hath not called us unto uncleanness but unto holiness"*

14. **LASCIVIOUSNESS:** This is vital urge for sexual intercourse. It is also called libido, sexual impulse, lustful lewdness, concupiscence, chambering or wantonness

15. **LICENTIOUSNESS:** "LICENTIOUSNESS" comes from the English word license and licentiousness means indulging in excessive freedom of sexual intercourse; giving to the indulgence of animal passion.

This is lack of self-control of one's sexual desire. No inhibition of one's immoral desires. It leads to many other forms of immorality such as child abuse, masturbation, bestiality and so on.

16. **PROMISCUITY:** This is indulging in indiscriminate sexual intercourse, a confused immoralist without order, distinction, choice or taste.

This group can sleep with a mad man or woman, with a man or woman of hundred years, with an under aged person or even with anybody from any walk or section of life. No choice, no taste, no order, anything male/ female goes, it is a mixture without order of distinction. It is the easiest and fastest way of spreading S.T.D

17. **LESBIANISM:** This is a woman with another as with a man to derive sexual pleasure. They normally start this habit in secondary schools, in female schools in the dormitories; the older girls take the new and younger girls as their pet. They sleep together and derive sexual pleasure. Some that could not drop the habit after secondary school, continued with it and gradually they lose interest in men and crave for other women for their sexual needs. At the early stage, it is called PETTING.

18. **HOMOSEXUALITY:** This means man sleeping with another man in order to derive sexual pleasure. A man lying carnally with another man as with a woman

In Leviticus 18:22 God commanded

"Thou shall not lie with mankind as with womankind, it is abomination"

In chapter 20:13 of Leviticus, God commanded that men guilty of this sin should be put to death and their blood shall be upon them.

In European and American countries today, there are men-prostitutes as they have women prostitutes, Homosexuality has spread so wide and it is welcomed among them. Men sell their bodies as women do in brothels. And recently one religious community has welcomed them in their midst by ordaining one of them as bishop. Instead of banishing him, they honoured, glorified and promoted him. Evil of the last days.

Another name for a homosexual is GAY.

Gay liberation is the freeing of homosexuals from social disadvantages and prejudice. This one done by the religious group in Europe, what will it be called? Religious Gay liberation perhaps, God is angry with mankind and His wrath will soon be poured upon the children of disobedience.

Apostle Paul in 1 Corinthians 6:9 called them ABUSERS OF THEMSELVES WITH MANKIND. He grouped them together with other ugly faces of immorality such as fornicators, idolaters, adulterers and effeminate and warned that such people will not inherit the kingdom of God.

19. **BISEXUALITY:** This is a group of people that are hermaphroditic in nature. They are attracted sexually to both sexes and can go into immorality with any sex. Hermaphrodites are animals or human beings with sexual organs of the male and female at the same time.

20. **ORAL SEX:** This is the act of having sexual intercourse with the use of the mouth. There are two types of oral sex. CUNNILINGUS AND FELLATIO.

Cunnilingus is the oral stimulation of the female genitals, the use of tongue to make the woman reach orgasm while fellatio is the oral stimulation of the male genital, the sucking of the male organ by the female for him to reach climax.

Any form of oral sex either cunnilingus or fellatio pollutes the tongue and makes one's prayer powerless, the power of the tongue is destroyed, it is paraphilism.

21. **ANAL SEX:** This is having sexual intercourse through the anus. It is also called SODOMY. God hates it with perfect hatred and for this, He destroyed Sodom and Gomorrah with fire and brimstone, and He warned in.

Deuteronomy 23:17

"Thou shall be no whore of the daughters of Israel, NOR A SODOMITE of the sons of Israel"

This is what the homosexuals do. The gay people are abusers of themselves with mankind.

Moreover, that you are legally married to your wife does not give you the license for paraphilism such as oral sex or anal sex. The word sodomy comes from the name of a city Sodom, well known for their immorality.

When three Angels came to Lot, the whole men of Sodom besieged the house of Lot asking him to bring the three men out for them that they may "know" them. That is, that they would lie carnally with them as if they were women. God destroyed that city for their sodomy.

Today we have cities worse, more corrupt, dead in immorality more than Sodom and Gomorrah. Cities like Soho before Soho was the sex Centre of the world but today, Italy ranks No 1, Hollywood, Ojuelegba in Lagos etc. are other examples. I know of a locality in Nigeria where most girls must practice prostitution before getting married.

22. **GROUP SEX:** This is organized sex party. It is also called orgy: where everybody comes to the party with nightgown or pyjamas with nothing under and everybody is free to indulge in sex. This is done in occult societies. Church of Satan and other satanically inspired organizations and groups.

23. **SWINGING:** This is also a group sex but here, partners are exchanged.

24. **POLYGAMY:** This is the act of marrying more than one wife. There are morally debased men that are not satisfied with one woman and they legally marry other women. Society accepts polygamy but God does not accept it. It pulled king Solomon down and God in the book of Deuteronomy 17, warned us not to have more than one wife.

"Neither shall he multiply wives to himself that his heart turn not away "

If you are looking for families where arrows and spiritual bullets and other forms of missiles are going on day and night, go to polygamous families. There is perpetual war, unending crisis, jealousy, evil rivalry, witchcraft attacks, unhealthy competition, household wickedness and every other form of evil you can think about go to polygamous families.

The first polygamous man in the Bible was a murderer. The first murderer and the first wizard were Cain. The second murderer and the second wizard were the polygamist called Lamech, great grandson of Cain, he married two wives Adah and Zillah.

Spiritual science has proven that every polygamist is a wizard because by the time he marries one, two, three one of them must be a witch, and sleeping with a witch every night and eating her food every day makes one a wizard automatically. Polygamy is immoral, if one wife is not enough, two or even one thousand like Solomon will still not be enough.

25. **POLYANDRY:** This is the act of a woman having more than one husband at a time and having children for them, some people in certain stages of civilization did allow it.

Today this is done even in some parts of Nigeria. A woman living with her husband will introduce her man friend to her husband and the man friend will now bring one goat and some drinks and kola nuts and the friendship will be legalized. Any time the woman needs her man friend, she will go from her husband's house to her man friend and spend the night it is called "Agili" among the people.

Amongst the Inuit culture, once they have a visitor, the highest form of hospitality a husband will offer to the visitor is his wife, especially if their visitor is going to spend the night.

There is still another part of Nigeria where a woman can marry up to ten husbands and have children for all. Jesus told the woman of Samaria at the well that she has had five husbands and the present one she was living with was like the previous ones. None was her husband. She was living in sin.

26. **GIGOLOO:** This is a situation where a young man is living at the expenses of an older woman. The old woman takes care of

the young man financially while the young man satisfies her sexual desires. Sometimes it may lead to marriage.

27. **GIGOLETTER:** This is a young woman living at the expenses of an older man. The old man furnishes her with everything she needs while the young woman satisfies his sexual desires. Sometimes it may lead to marriage. A young girl marrying an old man because of his money and other things she can get out of the man.

28. **PAEDERASTY:** This is a sexual relation of a male with a male especially a male child or a boy. This is also called CHILD ABUSE.

29. **PAEDOPHILIA:** This is sexual desire whose object are children. This is also called CHILD ABUSE.

30. **TRANSVESTITE:** This refers to people who dress in the clothes of the opposite sex. People may be wondering whether this is another ugly face of immorality. Yes, it is, because God made it clear in the scriptures that people should not do this. But some people claim to be wiser and more knowledgeable than God. Their argument is that it does not matter. Whatever God says matters.

In the book of Deuteronomy God commanded...

> *"The woman shall not wear that which pertaineth unto a man. Neither shall a man put on a woman's garment. For all that do so are abomination unto Lord thy God." Deuteronomy 22:5*

I urge you ladies and some old women who are wearing trousers, repent, and you men dressing in women's wears repent. Paul in

1 Corinthian 6:9 calls the men that do this EFFEMINATE. He warns that they shall not inherit the kingdom of God.

31. **TRANSSEXUAL:** This is a person anatomically of one sex and apparently normal physically but having an abnormally strong desire to belong to the opposite sex.

It is one who has a surgical treatment to alter the external sexual features so that they resemble those of the opposite. This is called TRANSSEXUALISM, SEX CHANGE OR SEX REVERSAL

32. **PIMP:** This is one who procures gratifications for the lust of others. It is one who lives with and sometimes solicits for a prostitute and lives off her earnings.

The pimp organises customers for the prostitute and receives the wages themselves and pays the prostitutes their wages as much or as little as they choose to, or nothing at all.

It is also called A PANDER/PANDERESS OR FANCY MONGER

33. **LUST OF THE EYES:** This is the desire of one to look on, feeding the eyes on the things that do not edify one.

The eyes are greedy. They like looking at things that are spiritually ugly. The eyes are the major cause of immorality. The eyes see and the heart desires the mouth speaks, and the legs walk to carry it out.

The Bible warned in 1 John 2:16...

> "For all that is in the world the lust of the flesh and the lust of the eyes..."

Jesus also warned that it is better to pluck out one's eyes and make heaven than to have two eyes feeding on evil and go to hellfire.

It is what you look at that goes into your life and that is what you meditate on and that is what you bring out. Peter in 2 Peter 2:14 put it this way:

> "Having eyes full of adultery and that Cannot cease from sin beguiling Unstable souls..."

This group of people undress the opposite sex with their eyes and imagine and fantasize how they will be on bed. This is immorality of the heart. Jesus said that if you look and lust, you have already done it in your heart.

34. **LUST OF THE FLESH:** This is when one is burning with evil passion. The flesh is hungry not for food but for sexual intercourse. The flesh desires evil sexual pleasures and pulls one towards it. For those that are already caged, rest will disappear, sleep will fly away, and the flesh will be crying for gratification. The individual will now begin to look for a way out. Sometimes they go to prostitutes, sometimes it is their girlfriends, sometimes it is masturbation, whatever it is, it is immorality.

After the evil has been done, they rest for a while before the ugly desire rears its ugly head again.

"For all that is in the world, lust of the flesh..." John 2:16

For a child of God to make heaven, the flesh must die, if the flesh is alive to sin the person is deceiving himself in the Christian race because the flesh will be a stumbling block on the way. He must pray and deal with the flesh. Mortify the flesh, crucify the flesh, kill the flesh, do away with carnality and begin to walk in the spirit.

35. **RAPE:** This is unlawful sexual intercourse usually by force with another person without that person's consent. A lot of things can cause this, mode of dressing of the victim, or lack of self-control of the attacker and so on.

36. **NYMPHOMANIA:** This is defined as morbid and uncontrollable sexual desire in women. This group cannot be satisfied sexually, so they continue looking for where to get satisfaction.

37. Their desire for sex is uncontrollable and this desire cannot be satisfied which makes them lose interest in men and they become lesbians and still their desire cannot be satisfied by their fellow women which lead to frustration.

38. This Nymphomania is a type of madness about sexual pleasure. The more they indulge in it the more they want it, during this stage of frustration, if they are not delivered; they enter final destructive stage of suicide.

39. They always end up killing themselves because they have the type of sexual desire which no man or woman can satisfy. She is also called a sex maniac.

40. **SUGAR DADDY:** This is a Nigerian English name for those old men who go after primary and secondary school girls young enough to be their grandchildren.

They keep them and sleep with them and furnish them with money. This is an opposite of Gigolette.

41. **SUGAR MUMMY:** This is also a Nigerian English name given to those rich old women that cannot be satisfied by their old and weak husbands. They seek out strong and energetic young boys and keep them to satisfy their sexual desires while taking care of them financially and lavishing them with presents. It is the opposite of gigolo.

42. **CONCUBINAGE:** This is the living together of two unmarried people with the belief that they will soon get married.

This is living in sin. Premarital sexual relationship is immorality. Many ladies even some children of God, once any man mentions marriage into their ears, they park their loads and go to live with the man in his house. No introductions, no bride price, no traditional marriage, no white/Christian wedding and before you know it, it is pregnancy.

Many are living with their so-called husbands today whereas they are not legally married. They are living in sin.

I know a couple with four children, though the traditional marriage was done but all my effort to get them wedded in the Church was abortive even after promising to foot the bill of all the expenses that will be incurred. They did not understand.

43. **SLEEPING WITH A WOMAN DURING HER MENSTRURAL CYCLE:** There are many men that have no restraint on their part, no self-control. Any time they desire sex, even if their wives are undergoing their menses, they will

41

still sleep with them. This is dangerous to their health and moreover God warned against it.

"Also, thou shall not approach unto a woman to uncover her nakedness as long as she is put apart for her uncleanness" Leviticus 18:19

44. **INORDINATE AFFECTION:** This is unrestrained excessive and inordinate affection that deviates from the rule and correct order of things. The simple word for this is infatuation. This means turning to folly deprived of judgment and inspired with foolish passion.

This leads to rape, wrong choice of marriage partners marital troubles and finally divorce. At the initial stage, the person will be blind with foolish passion, after some time it may be after marriage, his\her eyes will become cleared and whatever he/she saw before will not be there again and this will breed problems, frigidity, troubles and divorce.

Paul in Colossians 3:5 advised us thus:

"Therefore, mortify your members which are upon the earth, fornication uncleanness, INORDINATE AFFECTION evil concupiscence and covetousness which is idolatry."

45. **DIVORCE:** This is the legal dissolving of the marriage between a husband and a wife.

The Bible is against it. Jesus says that if any man divorces his wife and marries another that he and the new wife are committing adultery and if any man marries a divorced woman, they are also committing adultery.

"But I say unto you that whosoever shall Put away his wife saving for the case of fornication caused her to commit Adultery and whosoever shall marry Her that is divorced committeth adultery"

46. **ELOPEMENT:** This is the running away of two lovers to get married secretly. There is a type of elopement called RAPACITY. This is to seize and carry off. I know an area in Nigeria where a married woman can agree with her man friend and they elope by night. The following day the news will spread that he had carried her and ran away.

This means that he has taken her from her husband and now the woman in question here will become the wife of the man that took her by night and ran away. You cannot covet another man's wife, and before this elopement, they must have been sleeping together secretly before it came to the point of elopement.

47. **IMMORALITY OF HE HEART:** This means dwelling on impure sexual thoughts of divers types. Jesus says that he who looks at a woman to lust after her has already committed immorality with her in his heart. Another name for it is IMAGINATION OR FANTASIZING. This is the conceiving of the mental images of sexual acts which is not really realized. It is the forming of sexual images in one's mind. Read Matthew 5:27

48. **CONSTANT SEXUAL DREAMS:** There are people that claim to be holy, no boyfriend, no girlfriend but every night they have sex in the dream. This action pollutes one's spirit and defiles the person.

There are two types of INCUBUS AND SUCCUBUS. SPIRIT HUSBAND is known as INCUBUS. This is sexual demon from the waters that comes to sleep with women at night.

Genesis 6:1-4 has a record of spiritual beings that came on errand and instead of minding their business they started sleeping with the daughters of men. Spirit husbands can be inherited, and a lady can open a door to them through her mode of dressing, patronizing native doctors, white garment prophets and sexual immorality or going to offer sacrifice and bath in the river.

SPIRIT WIFE is known as SUCCUBUS. As we have spirit husbands, so do we have spirit wives. These are female sexual spirit beings that fancy men and come to them as their wives to sleep with them anytime they desire.

The aftereffects of having sex in the dream are many and catastrophic in nature. Among them are evil deposits, fibroid, late marriage or no marriage, troubled marriage, bareness, spiritual children, death of earthly spouse, vagabond children miscarriage, lack of peace etc.

Witches can develop male organs in order to have sex with fellow women in their sleep. For both spirit husband and spirit wife attacks the way of escape is deliverance (For details, see Activities of spirit husband and wife by the same author).

49. **NECROPHILISM:** This is a morbid liking for dead bodies, having a sexual attraction or intercourse with a dead person.

Some armed robbers once attacked a home and killed a woman at the house. As others were busy carrying away the properties, one of them was busy having sex with the dead woman.

50. **FETISHISM:** This is a pathological attachment of sexual interest to an inanimate object, the worship of a fetish power and strong belief in charms.

51. **NUDISM:** This is the practice of going naked. God does not like it and that was why he killed an animal and covered Adam and Eve when the glory of God left them, and they were naked.

There are some people within Nigeria who when they are celebrating one evil festival in honour of one demon of the area, all the young ladies will come out naked.

In the Republic of Benin and in Togo, there are some women dedicated to idols and they do not wear anything, they just walk about naked. This can cause evil attraction, rape, fornication or any other type of immorality. It is exhibition of the highest order.

52. **FILTHY COMMUNICATION:** This refers to immoral words, dirty and unclean words or jokes that are not expected within Christian fold. Jesus rightly warned that what comes out of a man is what defiles a man. If your words, your communication is immoral, you are in the category of those that have committed immorality of the heart because the Bible says that out of the abundance of the heart the mouth speaketh.

"But now ye also put off all these Anger, wrath, malice, blasphemy, Filthy communication out of your mouth"

And Peter in 2 Peter 2, was talking about Sodom and Gomorrah. How immoral they were, how they vexed Lot with their filthy conversation.

53. **INCEST:** This is sexual intercourse within the prohibited degree of kindred. God is profoundly serious with man's sexual relationship and he carefully brought out in details incestuous sexual relationship that must be avoided. In Leviticus 18:6-18 He says:

> *"None of you shall approach to any*
> *That is near of kin to him to uncover*
> *Their nakedness, I am the Lord. The*
> *Nakedness of thy father or the*
> *Nakedness of thy mother shall*
> *Thou not uncover.*

> *The nakedness of thy father's wife*
> *Shall thou not uncover, it is thy father's*
> *Nakedness. The nakedness of thy*
> *Sister the daughter of thy mother whether*
> *She be born at home or abroad even their*
> *Nakedness thou shall not uncover*
> *The nakedness of thy son's daughter*

> *Or of thy daughter's daughter even*
> *Their nakedness thou shall not uncover*
> *For theirs is thine own nakedness*
> *The nakedness of thy father's wife's*
> *Daughter begotten of thy father, she*
> *Is thy sister, thou shalt not uncover*
> *The nakedness of thy father's sister*

She is thy father's near kinswoman
Thou shat not uncover the nakedness
Of thy mother's sister, for she is thy
Mothers near kinswoman
Thou shalt not uncover the nakedness
Of thy father's brother. Thou shalt not
Approach to his wife, she is thy aunt
Thou shalt not uncover the nakedness

Of thy daughter in-law, she is thy son's
Wife thou shalt not uncover her
Nakedness. Thou shalt not uncover
The nakedness of a woman and her
Daughter, neither shall thou take thy sons

Daughter or thy daughter's daughter to
Uncover her nakedness for thy are thy
Near kinswoman. It is wickedness
Neither shalt thou take a wife to her sister
To vex her to uncover her nakedness
beside the other in her life time"

What the Lord is saying in the above passage is that no woman shall have sexual intercourse with her father, brother, uncle, son, half-brother, nephew, son in-law brother in-law, grandfather, stepson or stepfather or grandson. And no man shall sleep with his mother sister aunt, daughter, niece, daughter in-law, sister in-law mother in-law, grandmother, stepmother or stepdaughter or granddaughter.

But this commandment has since being violated by mankind, men sleep with their daughters, uncles with their nieces and mothers with their sons, brothers sleeping with their sisters, mother's in-law with some sons' in-law. There is no more restraint and restriction, today men live like beast and the wrath of God will soon be poured upon the earth.

Fathers have gotten children from their daughters; sisters have been impregnated by their brothers and mothers by their sons. The Earth is now worse than Sodom and Gomorrah. However, Paul in the book of Romans 1:21-32 says:

> *"Because that when they knew God, they*
> *Glorified Him not as God neither were*
> *Thankful but became vain in their*
> *Imaginations and their foolish hearts were*
> *Darkened. Professing themselves to be*
> *Wise they became foolish. And changed the*
> *Glory of the incorruptible God into an image*
> *Made like to corruptible man and to birds*
> *And four-footed beasts*
> *And creeping things wherefore God also*
> *Gave them up to uncleanness through the*
> *Lusts of their own hearts to dishonor their*
> *Own bodies between themselves who*
> *Changed the truth of God into a lie and*
> *Worshipped and served the creature more*
>
> *Than the creator who is blessed forever more*
> *Amen. For this cause, God gave them up*
> *Into vile affection for even their women did*

48

Change the natural use into that which is
Against nature. And likewise, also the men
Leaving the natural use of the women.

Burned in their lusts one toward another
Men with men working that which is
Unseemly and receiving in themselves that
Recompense of their error which was meet

And even as they did not like to retain God
In their knowledge; God gave them over to
A reprobate mind, to do those things which
Are not convenient, Being filled with all
Unrighteousness, fornication, wickedness
Covetousness, maliciousness, full of envy
Murder, debate, deceit, malignity whispers
Backbiters, haters of God, despiteful, proud,
Boasters, inventors of evil things,
Disobedient to parents, without natural
Affection, implacable, unmerciful, who
Knowing the judgment of God that they
Which commit such things are worthy of
Death, not only do the same but have
Pleasure in them that do them"

Pray all these prayer points in Jesus' name and pray with aggression, violence and anger.

1. Every foundational bondage of immorality from my father's house and from my mother's house die in Jesus' name

2. Every spirit of fornication and adultery in my family line, I cut you off

3. You spirit of unfaithfulness in my life, die by fire in Jesus' name

4. You my flesh, you will not take me to hell fire in Jesus' name

5. You my flesh I dethrone you, be mortified in Jesus' name

6. You my eyes, be delivered from lust in Jesus' name.

7. You the foreskin of my heart, be circumcised in Jesus' name

8. You the prostitute assigned to trap me die in Jesus' name

9. You my Bathsheba, my David will not see you in Jesus' name

10. You Delilah you will not shave the hair of my Samson in Jesus name

11. You Jezebel targeting my life, fail woefully in Jesus' name

12. Any lap trap set for me, catch your owner in Jesus' name

13. Any agent of Satan assigned to seduce me, fail woefully in Jesus' name

14. Any spell of immorality cast upon me, break and die in Jesus' name

15. Any lie of the devil working against my life, be exposed in Jesus' name

16. Any spirit wife/husband polluting my life die.

17. Blood of Jesus cleanse me from every incestuous sin in Jesus' name

18. Every evil blood covenant of immorality, break and die in Jesus' name

19. Any curse working against my life, break and die in Jesus' name.

20. Every evil soul-tie with my past girl/boyfriends break in Jesus' name

CHAPTER FOUR

∽

Causes Of Sexual Immorality

"The mouth of a strange woman is a deep pit, he that is abhored of the lord shall fall therein" Proverbs 22:4

T here are two main causes of sexual immorality. We have SPIRITUAL and PHYSICAL causes.

SPIRITUAL CAUSES: Spiritually men and women are manipulated, remote-controlled or possessed with the spirit of sexual pervasion. People are manipulated the rough one way or the other to commit adultery. Dr. Olukoya in one of his sermons told us about a young man that was born in a herbalist's home. The parents of the child were so poor they could not pay. On the day of circumcision, the herbalist asked for his money, but they could not pay, so the herbalist took the foreskin of the child and cast it into his shrine with a curse that because the parent did not give him his money, the boy will be causing trouble with his manhood always.

At the age of puberty, at a very tender age, the boy started causing trouble with his manhood. The young girls in his neighbourhood and other young girls close to him, before one could know what was going on, all the young girls were pregnant. The young girls in his street, the young girls in his school, none of them were spared, so every day, parents of these girls were coming with their pregnant daughters one after another to see and know who is responsible. Some came with the new-born babies, but when they see the small boy that was responsible, they became more confused.

When the parents of the boy became tired of these problems, they started looking for solution and that was how they came to Mountain of Fire and Miracles Ministries and through prayers the Holy Spirit revealed the source of the problem. There are some angels of darkness that are responsible for sexual sins.

SATAN:

As a student of J.P Timmons, I learnt that Satan has spiritual satellite control system and through this system, he projects thoughts and images into the minds of human beings. So, when you suddenly begin to think impure thoughts, unholy thoughts, know that Satan is at work in order to make you to sin. He will flash pictures that will seduce you and put evil desires in you. If you entertain such thoughts and do not pray them out immediately, you will see yourself committing that sin.

When your mind is being bombarded constantly with thoughts of immorality you can be sure Satan has his satellites systems focused on you. The thought of immorality, if not pushed out or prayed away from one's mind, could dwell there until it germinates and bears evil fruits.

ABADDON:

Abaddon is a Hebrew word which means eternal destruction. J.P Timmons described him as a tall black and foul-smelling demon.

He is also called polluting demon. His aim is to pollute humans. He was the brain behind rising the discotheques throughout the whole world to encourage sexual immorality. He was responsible for the invention of "disco halls".

Abaddon is behind rock music. His works include:

- Adultery
- Fornication
- Incest
- Homosexuality
- Lesbianism
- Bestiality
- Masturbation
- Pornography
- Peadophilism
- Alcoholism
- Lust of the Eyes
- Lust of the flesh
- Drug Addiction
- Smoking
- Prostitution
- Nymphomania
- Materialism
- Divorce
- Gluttony
- Lying
- Abortion
- Murder

There are many other evil immoral habits Abaddon is responsible for in the lives of men and he drives people into sin of filth in order to make them unclean and impure before God and he also tries to keep away from repenting. He was behind the activities of Jezebel of Thyatira.

Through sexual sins, he puts his victims into more bondage. This principality called Abaddon has a co-worker who works hand in hand with him and he has his area of specialization too.

ASMODEE:

According to J.P Timmons this fallen angel also called the stinker. His appearance is that of a fat and smelly demon-looking man. He is tall in stature and walks very lightly with a spring in his step and he also have wings. Asmodee is heavily involved with sexual immorality and marries people for Satan. He is responsible for the spirit of Jezebel in the Churches.

He works with Abaddon, Leviathan and other marine powers such as water spirit and queen of the coast and he causes marriage problems. He works against marriage institution in Christian families.

His works include:

♦ Attacking and killing the prophets of God
♦ Sending Jezebellian agents to the churches
♦ Prostitution
♦ Pornography
♦ Homosexuality
♦ Lesbianism
♦ Masturbation
♦ Incest
♦ Bestiality
♦ Incest
♦ Child abuse
♦ Bareness of the womb
♦ Marital problems

- Late marriage
- Divorces
- Inability to marry.
- Miscarriage
- Death of children
- Spirit wife
- Spirit husband
- Breakdown of morals by Christian couples
- Jealousy
- Adultery
- Vagabond children
- Recruiting of young girls to seduce ministers of God.

Those girls who stay long in this business become lesbians, and if they are not arrested and delivered by the Holy Ghost, they become Nymphomaniacs who finally become frustrated because of unsatisfied sexual desire and they end up committing suicide.

QUEEN OF HEAVEN:

This power is also known as Ashtaroth the wife of Baal which came from Babylon. She is one of the fallen angels. She resides in the second heaven with her headquarters on the moon. She is being worshipped throughout the whole world and some religious groups worship her in ignorance, thinking they are honouring Mary the mother of Jesus Christ.

Queen of heaven is the woman, God is referring to in Jer.7:18 and Jer.44:17-25, God is angry with her worshippers. She has different names in different countries of the world but the religious sect that worships her calls her.

- The mother of God
- Queen of heaven
- Holy mother
- Our Lady of Fatima
- Our Lady of Lourdes
- The mediatrix of all grace
- Madonna
- Health of the sick
- Queen of the Apostles
- Virgin Mary
- The Gate of Heaven
- Ark of the Covenant and so on.

When you get hold of their simple prayer booklet, you will see the litany of the Blessed Virgin Mary. All these titles are the names by which this Queen of Heaven is known in this religious circle. Her major works include:

- Confusion
- Violence
- Bloodshed
- Murder
- Witchcraft
- False Religion

- Hatred for true Christianity
- Hatred for the true word of God
- Massacre of the true believers in the form of inquisition
- Ancestral worship
- Causing of accidents
- Untimely deaths
- Rioting
- Prostitution
- Sexual lust
- Pornography
- Homosexuality
- Lesbianism
- Adultery
- Fornication
- Group sex
- Incest
- And many other evil works.

Queen of heaven always keeps her worshippers in an extraordinarily strong bondage. She causes religious blindness and religious bondage. She is very wicked. She does not release her captives if not by great violent prayers, followed by series of deliverance programs.

For detailed information on this woman, Queen of heaven, get a copy of the End Time Army of the Lord by the same author.

SPIRIT O BELIAL:

Belial is one of the strongmen in the Bible. Belial means valueless, vile cheap, worthless, ungodly, good for nothing, evil. The children of Belial refer to some people under the control and influence of Belial.

It is the spirit that leads people astray.

It is the spirit of error. It leads people away from the Lord. It has so much seductive power.

What happened in Genesis 19:4-9 was influenced by the spirit of Belial. The men of Sodom, all came out and forcefully desired to have a carnal knowledge of the men that visited Lot.

In 1 Kings 21:9-13 These men of Belial were hired bear false witness against Naboth. Jezebel, wife of Ahab masterminded the plan.

In Deuteronomy 13:12-13 God is warning His people that anytime the children of Belial will want to mislead them into worshiping strange gods, let them never agree.

In the book of Judges 19:22-30 the drama that look place in Lots house in Sodom was re-enacted here. In Lots house, they failed because those visitors were Angels. They were not ordinary men but here they succeeded. They demanded to have a carnal knowledge of a man, a stranger that was sojourning with an old man in the city but eventually they ended up in raping the strangers, concubine to death.

> *"Now as they were making their hearts*
> *Merry behold the men of the city, certain*

Sons of Belial beset the house round about
And beat at the door and spake to the master
Of the house, the old man saying, bring
Forth the man that came into thine house
That we may know him" Judges 19:23

The spirit of Belial also operates through alcoholism and drunkenness. In 1 Samuel 1:16, Hannah was telling Eli the priest not to count her as a daughter of Belial because Eli thought she was drunk.

In 1 Samuel 2:12 the Bible says

"Now the sons of Eli were sons of Belial they know not the Lord"

Verse 22 now explains why they are sons of Belial

"Now Eli was very old and heard all that His sons did unto all Israel and how they Lay with women that assembled at the Tabernacle of the congregation"

The spirit if Belial is a spirit of rebellion, a spirit that insults the glory of God.

In 2 Samuel 20:1 it is recorded.

"And there happened to be there a man Of Belial whose name was Sheba the Son of Bichri, a Benjamite and he blew a Trumpet and said we have no part in David Neither have we inheritance in the son of Jesse. Every man to his tent O Israel"

Belial is one of the four principalities. Others are Apollyon, Abaddon and the Beast. These four are members of the supreme military council of Satan. They are ruling the four kingdoms of

Satan. Northern kingdom is in Moscow Russia, Southern kingdom is in Sidney Australia, Eastern kingdom is in Mecca city, Saudi Arabia while the western kingdom is in Vatican City, Rome Italy (For detailed information on these principalities and powers, get a copy of the End Time Army of the Lord by the same author).

In the book of 2 Corinthians 6:14-18. Paul the Apostle commanded the true children of God not to be unequally yoked together with unbelievers.

> *"For what fellowship hath righteousness*
> *With unrighteousness and what communion*
> *Hath light with darkness and what concord*
> *Hath Christ with Belial?"*

The works and operations of the spirit of Belial include:

- Disobedience
- Uncleanness, every unclean way, thoughts, money, actions, words etc.
- Adultery
- Rape
- Rebellion
- Prostitution
- Polygamy
- Polyandry
- Seduction
- Irreverence and Disrespect to God

- Error
- Leading of people astray
- Insulting of the Glory of God
- Alcoholism
- Addiction
- Sodomy
- Backsliding
- Fornication
- Oral Sex
- Incest
- Homosexualism
- Lesbianism
- Group sex, Orgy
- Greed
- False witness
- Covetousness
- Fighting against the Lord's anointed
- Distraction of Gods children from true worship.

Belial is an immensely powerful, wicked and dangerous spirit which can only be overcome with prayer, purity and praises unto God.

So, the spiritual causes of sexual immorality will be traced to Satan himself and to four of his chief angels, two principalities and two powers: Abaddon, Belial, Asmodee and Queen of heaven. These four have been assigned to corrupt the world with sexual immorality. Marine powers and the water spirits are working under Abaddon and Asmodee and Queen of the Coast. Queen of the coast is answerable to Queen of heaven. Christians must be extra careful when these forces are at work. Without much prayer and help of the Holy Spirit, you discover that before you gather your defences together, the deed has been done already. So, Satan and his evil spirits must be attacked in prayer for one to be free from sexual immorality.

- Satan
- Abaddon
- Asmodee
- Queen of heaven
- Spirit of Belial
- Incubus spirit husband
- Succubus spirit wife
- Queen of the coast
- Water spirits
- Marine powers
- Spirit of sexual pervasion
- Spirit of sexual immorality
- Spirit of lust
- Seducing spirits
- Spirit of Jezebel
- Spirit of Delilah
- Spirit of witchcraft

PHYSICAL CAUSES:

In as much as Satan and some of his fallen angels and some evil spirits are behind sexual immorality. There are also some sexual immoralities that emanate from so many physical actions such as:

♦ Adamic Nature

♦ Bad Foundation

♦ Evil family pattern

♦ Evil inheritance

♦ Bad friends

♦ Wrong Exposure to sex

♦ Reading of erotic novels

♦ Entertaining impure sexual thoughts

♦ Watching of Blue films and pornographic pictures as well as reading of lewd novels, and Magazines etc.

♦ Lack of self-control

♦ Indiscipline

♦ Lack of fear of God

♦ Foolishness

♦ Ignorance of the Punishment of suffering in hell

♦ Ignorance of the reward of Holiness and righteousness

♦ Ignorance of the after effect of immorality

♦ Ignorance of word of God

♦ Carnality

♦ Prayerlessness

- Carelessness
- Not being committed to one's Christian life.
- Too much freedom with the opposite sex
- Poverty, Lack and want
- Uninvited or unchecked Relationship between teenagers
- Acceptance of boyfriend/girlfriend relationship
- Divorce
- Love of money.
- Alcoholism
- Idleness
- Culture and the Society
- The environment
- Problematic marriage
- Curiosity
- Overconfidence
- Greed
- Conducive atmosphere, Apartments and Places
- Separation of married couples
- Troubled and unhomely homes
- Associating with Unbelievers
- Covetousness

Pray every prayer point in Jesus name and pray with violence and aggression.

PRAYER POINTS:

- Every evil arrow of impure thoughts dies in Jesus' name.
- I receive power to overcame Satan, the world and my flesh in Jesus' name.
- I will not be unequally yoked with unbelievers.
- Any unfriendly friend in my life be exposed and be disgraced in Jesus' name.
- Any witchcraft power manipulating me into immorality die.
- You my foundation receive Holy Ghost fire and be repaired.
- Any evil inheritance of immorality in my life be cut off.
- Any evil family pattern of immorality in my family line, my life is not your candidate, die by fire.
- My marriage, you will not be troubled in Jesus' name.
- My home you will be a home of peace and rest.
- My wife/husband will be my best friend and lover.
- Any power planning separation for me and my wife/husband die.
- Any power cooking divorce for my wife/husband and me fail woefully.
- Every overconfidence in my life die in Jesus' name.
- Every spirit of covetousness in my life die.

CHAPTER FIVE

∽

Effects Of Sexual Immorality

"For by means of a whorish woman, a man is brought to a piece of bread and the adultress will hunt for the precious life. Can a man take fire in his bosom nd his clothes not be burned? Can one go upon hot coals and his feet not be burned? So, he that goeth in to his neighbours wife whosoever toucheth her shall not be innocent... but whosoever committeth adultery with a woman lacketh understanding, he that doeth it destroeth his own soul. A wound and dishonour shall he get and his reproach shall not be wiped away..." Proverbs 6:26-25

".... He Goeth After Her Straight Way As An Ox Goeth To The Slaughter Or As A Fool To The Correction Of The Stocks Till A Dart Strike Through His Liver As A Bird Hasteth To The Snare And Knoweth Not That It Is For His Life... For She Hath Cast Down Many Wounded, Yea Many Strong Men Have Been Slain By Her. Her House Is The Way To Hell, Going Down To The Chambers Of Death" Proverbs7:21-27

"The Mouth Of A Strange Woman Is A Deep Pit He That Is Abhorred Of The Lord Shall Fall Therein" Proverbs 22:14

"Know Ye Not That You Are The Temple Of God And That The Spirit Of God Dwelleth In You? If Any Man Defile The Temple

Of God, Him Shall God Destroy For The Emple Of God Is Holy Which Temple Ye Are" 1 Corinthians 3:16-17

"And The Man That Committeth Adultery With Anothr Mans Wife Even He That Commiteth Adultery With His Neighbours Wife. The Adulterer And The Adulteress Shall Surely Be Put To Death"

"And The Man That Leith With His Father's Wife Both Of Them Shall Surely Be Put To Death. Their Blood Shall Be Upon Them. And If A Man Lie With His Daugher In-Law, Both Of Them Shall Surely Be Put To Death. ...If A Man Lie Wtih Mankind As He Lieth With A Woman... They Shall Surely Be Put To Death...And If A Man Takes A Wife And Her Mother... Both He And They Shall Be Burnt With Fire... And If A Man Lie With A Beast He Shall Surely Be Put To Death And Ye Shall Slay That Beast" Leviticus 20:10-21

As sexual immorality has spiritual and physical causes, so it has spiritual and physical evil effects. It has many evil effects. Sexual immorality is dangerous and deadly and opens door to witchcraft attack against our lives. It strengthens evil bondages, satanic yokes and demonic afflictions and it gives our enemy, the devil, a legal ground to oppress us. It also makes a child of God to come down to zero level and to start all over again, that is, if the grace of God is sufficient for that person.

Effects of sexual immorality are so deadly that Paul the Apostle spent much time warning Christians to flee from it. Through sexual immorality, the Holy Spirit is grieved. His fire quenched His anointing frustrated and God's blessings blocked. Whatsoever we did with our body, we shall receive a reward. And it is good to point out here that sexual immorality has no single good effect. Jesus tells us in the book of John 6:63.

"It is the spirit that quickeneth The flesh profiteth nothing"

SPIRITUAL EVIL EFFECTS

Among the spiritual evil effects are:

1. **DESTRUCION BY GOD:** Apostle Paul made us to understand in 1 Corinthians 3:16-17 that those who defiled the temple of God shall be destroyed.

   "Know ye not that ye are the temple of God and that the spirit of God dwelleth In you? If any defile the temple of God Him shall God destroy. For the temple Of God is holy which temple ye are"
   1 Corinthians 3:16-17

2. **SPIRITUAL DEATH:** Sexual immorality causes spiritual death, eternal separation from God and loss of reward in heaven.

   "But fornication and all uncleanness... Neither filthiness...for this you know That no whoremonger nor unclean person... hath any inheritance in the kingdom of God..." 1 Corinthians 5:3-5

3. **FRAGMENTATION OF ONE'S SOUL:** Sexual immorality brings about the fragmentation of one's spiritual life and soul. The destiny is fragmented. The potential abilities and talents, virtues and gifts of such a person are fragmented and this leads to wastage, backwardness, stagnancy, sluggishness and satanic embargo on one's different areas of life.

4. **4. LACK OF PEACE AND FRUSTRATIONS:** Sexual Immorality blocks one's peace and opens door to frustration. Addiction to sex can turn one into a nymphomaniac who out of frustration stemming from unsatisfied sexual desire, commit suicide.

Moreover, young girls are always worried and anxious to see their menses the next month. After sleeping with their boyfriends, if they do not, peace will fly away and worry about what to do will take over.

5. **EVILBLOOD COVENANT:** Blood covenant is entered into through sexual immorality. A bond is made, and the two souls now become one spiritually. 1 Corinthians 6:15-19 says.

    "Know ye not that your bodies are The members of Christ? Shall I then The members of Christ and make Them the members of a harlot? God Forbid. What? Know ye not that he Which is joined to an harlot is one body For two saith he shall be one flesh? But He that is joined unto the Lord is one spirit". 1 Corinthians 6:15-17

6. **TRANSMISSION OF EVIL SPIRITS AND PROBLEMS:** During the act, evil spirits that are in the life of one partner are transmitted into the other. So, if one has only five demons oppressing him, by the time he finishes this immoral act, he may be having twenty, fifty, one hundred or one thousand demons depending on the number residing in his or her partner.

Problems are also transmitted too. Whatever problems the partners have are transmitted into each other so that if one has no problem at all, by the time he/she indulges in such act, problem from nowhere will enter the person's life.

7. **STENGHENS BONDAGES AND EVIL YOKES:** This act also strengthens bondages and evil yokes. It renews evil covenant in the lives of the victims.

If the person is already in a cage, he or she makes the cage more secured and tighter. if one is in a pit, the person makes the pit deeper. If the person is on evil alter, the person makes the evil alter more potent.

Sexual immorality empowers the enemy and supplies him weapons and makes the evil chain binding the person stronger.

8. **DIVERTS AND DESTROYS ONES DESTINY:** Those involved in this act can divert or even destroy their destinies completely. Joseph, the son of Jacob attained the height of a prime minster, "Major de Muar" in the land of Egypt because he feared God and overcame Potiphar's wife whom the devil wanted to use to destroy his destiny.

Reuben, the first son of Jacob, was replaced by Ephraim Joseph's son because Reuben slept with his father's wife and today, we hear of God of Abraham, Isaac and Jacob only because Reuben committed this abomination. If not, he should also be the God of Reuben.

Samson was not able to fulfil his destiny because of immorality. He went into prostitutes anytime his flesh demanded it. And Samson was a great man with a great ministry and because of immorality his destiny was diverted and destroyed, and he was not able to fulfil it.

9. **IT IS A SIN AGAISNT ONES OWN BODY:** The person sins against his/her own body. The person grieves the Holy Spirit and drives him away. The person defiles his/herself.

Paul warned us in 1 Corinthians 6:18

> *"Flee fornication, every sin that a man*
> *Doeth is without the body but he that*
> *Committed fornication sinneth against*
> *His own body"*

10. **IT DESTROYS ONE'S MINISTRY:** Samson's ministry was destroyed. Reuben's name and progenies are not remembered for good.

Many ministers today destroy their ministries through indulging in immorality. This immorality is the strongest weapon of the devil against ministers. After trying other pitfalls in vain, he will begin to send Jezebels and Delilahs to pull down the minister and to destroy his ministry. It takes the special grace of God for one to be entangled in the web of immorality to be delivered and to continue in the ministry.

11. **LOSS OF VIRTUES, POTENTIALS AND TALENTS:** The enemy uses this opportunity to steal away the virtues and buries the potentials. The person's gift will be paralyzed, dormant and wasted.

12. **BRINGS CURSES UPON ONE'S LIFE:** Deuteronomy 28:15-68 are curses pronounced unto people that disobey the commandment of God. God calls it abomination, confusion, uncleanness and wickedness.

Reuben received a curse from his father.

In Genesis 49:3-4 Jacob said:

> *"Reuben thou art my first born...unstable*
> *As water, thou shall not excel because thou*
> *Wentest up to thy father's bed then defiledst*
> *Thou it. He went up to my couch".*

In Leviticus 18:8 God says:

> *"The nakedness of thy father's wife shall*
> *Thou not uncover, it is thy father's*
> *Nakedness"*

This was the sin of Reuben and he received a curse from his father. He shall not excel

Deuteronomy 27:20-23 are some curses placed on some paraphiliacs. David murdered Uriah and married Bathsheba. He received a curse from God. Though he repented but the curse worked against him so much that.

♦ The child born by Bathsheba through the immoral union died.
♦ Ammon his son committed incest with his half-sister Tamar, both David's children.
♦ Absalom, because of this murdered Ammon
♦ Absalom himself slept with ten of his father's concubines on the rooftop were all Israel watched them.

- And Solomon son of Bathsheba set a record that no man can break. He married 700 wives and 300 concubines. A total of 1,000 women for one man and of cause the strangers among them diverted him away from the worship of the true God.

- Solomon killed Adonijah his brother because of Abisheg the Shunamite woman who as a young lady was brought to warm David's bed during his old age. because Adonijah requested to marry her.

13. **GIVES THE DEVIL A LEGAL GROUND:** This act also gives the devil a legal ground in one's life, a foothold to oppress a person. It is a ladder by which the devil climbs into one's life. It is an express invitation to troubles, problems, poverty, affliction, calamities, wretchedness and woes.

14. **OPENS DOOR TO SPIRIT HUSBANDS AND SPIRIT WIVES:** Through sexual immorality, spirit wives and husbands can gain entrance into one's life. When the person is sleeping, he will be having sex with unknown people in the dream.

15. **OPENS DOORS TO WITCHCRAFT ATTACK:** It also opens doors to witchcraft attacks. It strengthens their oppressions and their manipulations.

16. **DRIVES AWAY GODS PRESENCE AND PROTECTION:** Immorality is an abomination before God. So, He does not dwell in any place that is unclean and if God is not there, His protection is removed also.

17. **BLOCKS THE BLESSINGS OF GOD:** If one is living in immorality, God's blessings cannot locate the person.

18. **GOD WILLL NOT HEAR THE PERSON'S PRAYERS:** The Bible says that the prayer of a sinner is an abomination unto the Lord and the Psalmist in Psalm 66:18 says:

"If I regard iniquity in my heart The Lord will not hear me".

19. **PROVOKES GOD TO ANGER:** Immorality provokes God to anger. Ephesians 5:3-6 says.

"But fornication and all uncleanness...Neither filthiness nor foolish talking...Let no man deceive you...for because of These things cometh the wrath of God Upon the children of disobedience"

20. **MAKES SATAN HAPPY:** Immorality is a pit dug by Satan and anytime anyone falls into this pit, Satan rejoices because he has caught a victim.

21. **POLLUTES THE CHURCH:** Paul in Ephesians 5:3 warns that it should not even be mentioned among the saints because of its deadliness and evil effects. In the Church where the members do not live a holy life, where immorality is not avoided, the Church will be polluted, and the Holy Ghost will not move, and the power and the fire of God will not be manifest. The Church in Thyatira, Jesus tells them:

"Notwithstanding I have a few things
Against thee because thou sufferest
That woman Jezebel which calleth
Herself a prophetess to teach and to
Seduce my servants to commit
Fornication"
Revelation 2:20

22. **ETERNITY IN HELL FIRE:** The Bible also says in Revelation 21:8.

> *"But the fearful and the unbelieving and*
> *The abominable and murderers and*
> *Whoremongers and liars shall have*
> *Their part in the lake which burneth*
> *With fire and brimstone which is*
> *The second death"*

Spending eternity in hellfire is the worst thing that can happen to a human being and immorality is a bus whose destination is hellfire. Anyone in this bus can land in hellfire if the person does not jump out on time.

Galatians 5:19-21 says.

> *"Now the works of the flesh are manifest*
> *Which are these; Adultery, fornication*
> *Uncleanness, lasciviousness.... of*
> *Which tell you before... that they*
> *Which do such things shall not*
> *Inherit the kingdom of God"*

23. **THE AGONY OF NOT SEEING GOD:** Those dwelling in immorality shall not see God because the Bible says in

Hebrews 12:14

> *"Follow PEACE with all men and*
> *HOLINESS without which no eye*
> *Can see the Lord."*

The 23 points listed above are spiritual after-effects of immorality. There are many more but let us also jointly look at some physical after-effects which are many too.

PHYSICAL EFFECT EFFECTS

24. **UNWANTED PREGNANCY:** Sexual immorality can result to unwanted pregnancy.

25. **BREEDING OF BASTARDS:** Sexual immorality can lead to unwanted pregnancies which in turn lead to the breeding of bastards and a curse is automatically following all bastards. Except they repent and receive Jesus Christ, the curse which their mother brought upon them will be following them till their death. Look at what God says about bastards in the scriptures.

> *"Bastards shall not enter into the*
> *Congregation of the Lord. Even to*
> *His tenth generation shall he not*
> *Enter into the congregation of the Lord"*
> *Deuteronomy 20:2*

So those women breeding bastards are bringing problems and curses upon their children. Children begotten when you were in your father's house, when you were not yet married etc. are bastards.

26. **ABORTION:** When immorality results to unwanted pregnancy and the person involved is not ready for marriage or breeding of bastards, the next option is abortion and of course this is murder.

The spilled bloods of the unborn children are daily crying against their killers. Both the doctors and the nurses and the boy friends that financed the abortion and the woman with the unwanted pregnancy are all culprits and shall share in the punishment for murder. In some cases, the boyfriend/man friend will disappear, and the parents will take their daughter to an abortionist and remove the baby. They, the parents will share in the punishment.

27. **DAMAGE TO THE WOMB:** This abortion can lead to damage of the womb. Because of fear and lack of finance many of these women patronize quack-doctors and roadside chemist for abortion and in the process of this act, the womb may be damaged. Some patronize native doctors who prepare herbs that are deadly to the foetus. The foetus may die and decay in the womb thereby damaging vital reproductive organs.

28. **BARRENNESS:** Damage of the womb can result to barrenness. There are people that are barren today because during abortion, their wombs were removed with the babies in order to save their lives because of the complication that arose in the process.

29. **UNTIMELY DEATH:** Most of the time, the business of abortion results to untimely death. Many young girls have died in the process of committing abortion.

30. **MURDER:** Sexual immorality can result to murder of a human being. In the years gone by, two young men were fighting over a lady in one of the Nigerian universities and one was murdered. Also, in the nation's army, two generals had fought each other with guns because of a woman. Moreover, many men have died on strange women during immoral sexual acts.

31. **JEALOUSY:** Sexual immorality breeds jealousy. When one sees his/her sin partner moving with another person of the opposite sex, the eyes shall become red and heart ache shall set in and ungodly jealousy will manifest. Sometimes open challenge is thrown which leads to quarrelling and fighting and eventually to killing.

32. **LYING:** Sexual immorality makes the people that are involved to become professional liars. They can never be bold enough to tell their parents, guardians, wives or husbands about the immoral affair they are having.

33. **STEALING:** Sexual immorality has pushed many young men into armed robbery in order to satisfy their female sin partners financially.

34. **BAD EXAMPLE:** The act of immorality is a way of setting bad example to the children and to the young ones. As far back as 1985/86, when I was going for admission into the University of Benin, I stayed in a cousin's house who had three of his younger brothers living with him in one room. Every night, the man would go to bed with one or two of his girlfriends and the three younger brothers would sleep on the floor of the same room. This happened every night. So, when I noticed that it was his way of life, I called him and told him that he was free to sleep with as many as the number of women he desired if he did not want to repent but let his younger brothers never sleep in the same room with him anymore. I advised that his brothers could go to his neighbours' parlour any time he would come home with his prostitutes.

After this advice, my cousin told me never to come to his house whenever I come to Benin. Now that cousin is dead. He died of AIDS. He later married and his wife also died of AIDS and one of those younger brothers of his is also now dead.

35. **SPREADING OF S.T.D:** S.T.D. stands for sexual transmitted disease. There are many of them such as gonorrhoea, syphilis, Chlamydia and watts etc. as well as the incurable diseases called AIDS.

The sexually transmitted disease can cause bareness when they are chronic and untreated and can also lead to death when a deadly one like AIDS is contacted. As at now, AIDS has no known cure.

36. **WRONG MARRIAGE:** When a young girl gets into immorality and its results to unwanted pregnancy, if the family does not want to cover the shame by aborting the baby, they will quickly arrange a fast marriage between the girl and her sin partner.

The man may be truck pusher, a widower or an old man. There is no way this quickly arranged marriage will not lack love, peace, and joy.

37. **BREACH OF TRUST:** Immorality brings about breach of trust in the case of married couples. If one is involved in extramarital affair, the other partner will remove every trust he/she has on the partner.

38. **CAUSES HEATACHE TO SPOUSE:** Anyone involved in immorality breaks the heart of his/her spouse. This act causes great pain, which takes an exceptionally long time to heal. A

lot of misdeeds and errors can be easily forgiven in marriage, but it takes the special grace of God to forgive one who offends in this area.

39. **TROUBLED MARRIAGE:** Immorality brings trouble and problems into one's marriage. Peace, love, joy and happiness will fly away through the window once a strange man or woman comes in through the door.

The person involved will start staying outside late in the night and avoiding his or her married partner. The fellowship, relationship, communication and companionship will die.

40. **DIVORCE:** When the marriage is troubled and everything that makes marriage enjoyable is dead, the next stage is divorce, which is also another way of promoting immorality.

Jesus said that whosoever could marry a divorced person is committing adultery.

41. **POLYGAMY:** Immorality causes polygamy, many of these rich men that engage in extra-marital affairs normally add their sin parterres to the number of wives. If they have not tested the forbidden fruit, they would probably not think about marrying these strange women to their harem.

42. **POVERTY:** Immorality breeds poverty, where a man or woman is working, labouring and sweating in his/her endeavour and the proceeds will be handed over to the sin partner. Before the persons eye will be cleared, before the spells upon him/her will be removed, it will be too late for the person to plan his/her future. The person will be neck deep into the quagmire of

poverty. A Nigerian home movie entitled "Working for love" clearly illustrates this point and in the Bible, Solomon tells us in Proverbs 6:26

"For by means of a whorish woman a man Is brought to a piece of bread and the Adulteress will hunt to for the precious life"

43. **AN END TO ONE'S EDUCATION:** Immorality when it results to unwanted pregnancy, it can end one's education. This can lead to diversion of career or destiny which I have discussed before.

A young girl that was destined to be a medical doctor, because of unwanted pregnancy through immorality, stops her education at class four or five and marries a wine taper or a bricklayer or a gutter digger or a carpenter and she now sells "egwusi "and "ogbono" at the market in order to support her family. The girl's education has been terminated and her destiny diverted. There is no way again that girl can become a medical doctor if the Lord does not intervene.

44. **PROSTITUTION:** Sexual immorality leads to prostitution. When one desires one's sin partner and could not get him/her, the person can pick anyone available and addiction to sex makes many women to go into prostitution in order to have as many men as possible.

45. **UNFAITHFULNESS:** When one's marriage is faced with a lot of problems as a result of immorality, those forced into wrong marriages can decide to be unfaithful to their partners.

46. **THE RAGE OF THE CUCKOLDED MAN:** There is no limit to what a cuckolded man can do. In anger, he can kill

the man involved or burn down his house or kill his own wife or even his own children with the belief that they were gotten from outside. His wrath and anger take a divine intervention to be appeased.

47. **THE EMBARESSMENT OF THE BASTARDS:** In Igbo land, bastards are highly embarrassed. They have no home. As children, they will live in their mother's father's house. As adults, the entire village will revolt against them and ask them to go in search of their fathers.

A young man from my town is now facing such ordeal because his mother's cousin was responsible for the pregnancy. The mother later married an old man and took him along to her new home. Now he is a man married with children but has nowhere to call his home because his mother's husband's kinsmen have asked him to go and find his "square-root" and his mother's people know who his father is but cannot accept him because it is an abomination because his father and mother are first cousins. So, he is hanging between the devil and the deep blue sea. And what makes the whole matter so complicated is that his wife is also a bastard. If not, they should have found a home with his wife's people. Like begets like.

48. **TRUCE BREAKERS:** Immorality makes those involved in it to break their marital vows or the promise to marry later. When married people enter extra-marital after, they are breaking their marriage vows. The unmarried who are involved in immorality, out of infatuation on inordinate affection will quickly go into agreement to marry because in their little world they thought that they are the best for each other. With time, they will discover that the person they have agreed to

marry initially is now not good enough for them and they will marry another person.

Some have licked each other's blood and made a vow to marry each other and still broke the vows. Now they will be suffering the curse of a broken covenant.

49. **MANY CHILDREN FROM ONE WOMAN BY DIFFERENT MEN:** This makes the children to be of diverse evil character. Everyone will take after his father. Some will be very stubborn. Some will be armed robbers while some will be prostitutes.

50. **DECEPTION:** Immorality results to one deceiving the husband/wife, the bastard or even oneself.

PRAYER POINTS:

1. Every dream pollution of my life, be washed away by the blood of Jesus

2. Every defilement of my destiny, be cleansed by the blood of Jesus

3. Every satanic satellite control system working against me, scatter by fire

4. You spirit of Abaddon pursuing my life, die in Jesus name

5. Every work and operation of Abaddon in my life, die in Jesus name

6. Yokes and bondages of Abaddon over my life, be broken in Jesus name

7. You spirit of Asmodee, my life is not your candidate, die in Jesus name

8. Every projection from the marine world, die in Jesus name

9. Every marine power after my ministry, fall and die

10. You water spirit assigned to work against me fall and die

11. You spirit of Belial pursuing my life die

12. Every work and operation of Belial in my life, scatter in Jesus name

13. Every yoke and bondage of Belial over my life, break by fire

14. Every influence and control of spirit of Belial in any area of my life break and die

15. You leviathan spirit die by fire in Jesus name

CHAPTER SIX

~

28 Ways Out Of The Bondage Of Immorality

"My son, keep thy father's commandment andforsake not the law of thy mother, bind them continually upon thine heart and tie them about thy neck when thou goest, it shall lead thee when thou sleepest, it shall keep thee and when thou awakest it shall talk with thee for the commandment is a lamp and the law is light and reproofs of instruction are the way of life to keep thee from the evil women, from the flattery of the tongue of a strange woman" Proverbs 6:20-24

"My son keep my words and lay up my commandments with thee, keep my commanments and live and my laws as the apple of thine eye bind them upon thine fingers, write them upon the table of thine heart say unto wisdom thou art my sister and call understanding thy kinswoman that they may keep thee from the strange woman from the stranger which flattereth with her words" Proverbs 7:1-5

"My son give me thy heart and let thine eyes obersve my ways for a whore is a deep ditch, and a strange woman is a narrow pit she also lieth in wait as for a prey and increaseth the transgressors among men" Proverbs 23:26-28

"Shall the prey be taken from the mighty or the lawful captive delivered" But thus, saith the lord even the captives of the mighty shalll be taken away and the prey of the terrible shall be delivered for i will content with him that contendeth with thee and i will save thy children" Isaiah 49:24-25

T he Bible is our constitution. It is our guide, our law book; It is the oldest book and the most important book in the whole world.

Solution to every problem can be found in it no matter how stubborn, how serious and how chronic the problem has been.

Apostle Paul in many of his epistles gave us ways of escape from the bondages and yoke of immorality. Many men of God in the Bible gave pieces of advice that will help men and women to avoid and overcome immorality.

Jesus commanded that if it is the eye, hand, leg that will make us to go to hell fire, it is better for us to cut it off and enter heaven maimed than to enter hell fire whole.

The book of proverbs says that whosoever touches his neighbour's wife will never be guiltless. And what a cuckolded man will do can never be imagined.

Paul in 1 Corinthians 6:19-20 says.

"What? know ye not that your body is the temple of the Holy Ghost which is in you, which ye have of God and ye are are not your own for ye are bought with a price? Therefore glorify God in your body and in your spirit which are Gods"

In Galatians 5:16 Apostle Paul also says:

"This I say then walk in the spirit And you shall not fulfil the lust of the flesh"

In Ephesians 4:27 and 5: 3-4 he has this to say.

"Neither give place to the devil But fornication and all uncleanness Or covetousness let it not he once Named among you as becometh saints Neither filthiness nor foolish talking Nor jesting......."

Again in 1 Thessalonians 4:3 and 5:22 He also warns.

"For this is the will of God even Your sanctification that ye should Abstain from fornication"

"Abstain from all appearance of evil"

The above scriptures are admonitions by Paul for us to flee from immorality and live a holy life.

WAYS OF EXCAPE: For one to completely avoid immorality or break the bondage and yokes of immorality over one's live, these actions must be taken.

1. **SURRENDER TO OUR LORD JESUS:** This is the first action to take, surrender to Jesus and receive Him in your life as your personal Lord and Saviour. Be in Christ and let Christ be in you.

2. **REPENT AND CONFESS**: You must repent of the sins of immorality. Confess them to God. Ask for forgiveness and you will be forgiven. No matter how far and how deep you have

wallowed in the mud of immorality, with true repentance and total confession, God will forgive you.

3. **FORSAKE:** Now you must take another action of forsaking this sin of immorality. This is where the true test is based. Many may repent and confess this sin and afterwards, go back to it. To them, it is exceedingly difficult to break off but to very few courageous ones, they do forsake it, choosing Jesus rather than their sin partners. You must forsake it for the sake of heaven. Take a decision and make up your mind.

4. **RECOGNISE THAT YOU HAVE A PROBLEM:** You must stop telling yourself lies and recognize that really there is a problem about which you cannot help yourself and somebody more experienced in the Lord must help you. Then you will take another step forward

5. **GO FOR DELIVERANCE:** The Bible says

    "But upon Mount Zion shall be Deliverance there shall be holiness...." Obadiah 17

Without deliverance, it will be difficult to live a holy life. In fact, it will be impossible. It is deliverance first before holiness.

"That he would grant unto us, that We being delivered out of the hand Of our enemies might serve him Without fear in holiness and Righteousness before him all the Days of our lives" Luke 1:72 -75

When we are delivered, we serve Him without fear in holiness and righteousness, so go for deliverance.

6. **MAINTIAN THE DELIVERANCE:** Holiness and righteousness are not negotiable. You must maintain your deliverance by living a holy life.

7. **MORTIFY OUR MEMBERS:** Colossians 3:5 says.

   "Mortify therefore your members Which are upon the earth....."
   Your members are part of your body.
   You must bring all of them under control.
   Your eyes will not be allowed to feast on evil.
   Your tongue will not be allowed to speak evil.
   Your mouth will not be allowed to consume evil food.
   Your ears will not be allowed to listen to evil.
   Your mind will not be allowed to meditate on evil.
   Your heart will not be allowed to be taken over by evil.
   Your hand will not be allowed to touch or do evil.
   Your feet will not be allowed to go to any evil place.

8. **CRUCIFY YOUR FLESH:** Galatians 5:24 says

   "And they that are Christ's have crucified The flesh with the affections and lusts"

You must crucify your flesh. Die daily and nail yourself to the cross of Calvary and you will not obey the desires of the flesh because they are contrary to the desires of the spirit. Again, the book of John 3:63 says.

   "The flesh profiteth nothing It is the spirit that quickneth..."

9. **BE PRAYERFUL:** For you to come out of the bondage completely, you must be prayerful. I mean that serious warfare prayers must be undertaken by you. You must attack all the

powers behind sexual immorality. Jesus commanded that we pray so that we fall not into temptation.

10. **BE CAREFUL AND BE WATCHFUL:** You must be careful and watchful of the places you go, the people you relate with, your closeness with the opposite sex. Even when you think you are above it and cannot fall into such sin anymore, still be incredibly careful and watchful. That serious sister, that serious brother may be after you and before you can gather your defences, the deed has been done. Paul says.

"Wherefore let him that thinketh He standeth take heed lest he fall" 1 Corinthians 10:12

11. **RENEW YOUR MIND:** You must renew your mind through studying the word. Study the word of God. Memorize it, meditate on it, mumble it, that is, speak it to yourself silently, digest it, and hide it in your heart. Let it penetrate your spirit. Abide by it.

The word of God is Jesus Christ.

Jesus in you will destroy the power of sin. The Bible says

"And be renewed in the spirit of your Mind. And that you put on the new Man which after God is created in Righteousness and true holiness" Ephesians 4:23-24

12. **DESIRE GO IN YOUR HEART:** When you do this, you will give God your heart and your love. The fear of offending him because you love Him will not allow you to do anything that will hurt Him or grieve Him. No matter how tantalizing or how pleasant to the eyes. You must please God and no other.

Read Psalm 42:1-2, Proverbs 23:26

13. **CONTROL YOUR EYES:** Control your eyes so that you will not receive evil arrow in your heart. Remember what the eyes do not see the heart does not desire. Also remember that Jeremiah cried that his eyes affected his heart because he looked upon the daughters of the land. Control your eyes, it is especially important **for you to do so.**

14. **MIND WHERE YOU GO TO:** Dinah, Jacob's daughter was raped by the Prince of Shechem because she left her brethren and wandered away to the daughters of the land. If you go to where you are not supposed to go, God will not go with you and anything can happen to you there.

15. **TAKE A DECISION:** Make up your mind once and for all on this issue. Decide that you will not be entangled again in this bondage. Be determined and condition your mind never to dwell on thoughts of immorality.

16. **FASTING IS NECESSARY:** Occasionally go into fasting. Seek the face of God. Ask for His grace and mercy so that you will always prevail. Overcome and excel, moving forward in your relationship with God and not going back to sin of immorality.

17. **EXCERCISE SELF CONTROL:** Exercise self-control and be disciplined, even when sleeping with your spouse. Some men go into paraphilism with their wives such as anal intercourse called sodomy, oral sex either fellatio or cunnilingus, both are immoral and sleeping with her during her menses.

God warned against these practices, know that your body belongs to God so use it the way God wants.

18. **FOCUS YOUR MIND ON SPIRITUAL MATTERS:** Let your entire mind, aims and attention be fully given to God, to the works of God and to things pertaining to heaven and life after this one. In other words, be spiritually minded and live in the spirit and walk also in the spirit. Always meditate on your relationship with God.

19. **ALWAYS REMEMEBER THAT YOU CANNOT MANAGE HELL FIRE:** The pains of hell fire are unbearable and therefore cannot be managed. Anyone who dies in immorality will not escape the fire of hell.

20. **AVOID BAD COMPANIES:** Who are your friends? Those that can lure you into sin are bad friends and must be avoided at all cost. They are unfriendly friends. It was unfriendly friend Jonadab the son of Shimeah who advised Ammon the son of David to sleep with his half-sister, Tamar. Read 2 Samuel 13 and 2 Corinthians 6: 14-17.

21. **AVOID IDLENESS:** An idle mind is the devil's workshop. Avoid being idle. Occupy your mind with the word of God. Occupy your time with the work of God.

22. **AVOID TOO MUCH CLOSENESS WITH THE OPPOSITE SEX:** Avoid too much closeness so that you will not be magnetized into immorality.

23. **BE CONTENT WITH WHAT YOU HAVE:** Greed and covetousness are sins against God. Greed leads people especially women into immorality, so they sell their bodies and

with the proceeds buy what they desire. Covetousness makes men marry many wives and commit adultery and snatch other men's wives. Be content with what you have and wait for God to bless you the more.

24. **DRESS PROPERLY:** Dress properly so that you will not attract sexual demons and immoral men and women. Exhibitionism attracts sexual demons, immoral men and women. Dress properly to avoid being raped, to avoid being pressurized into sin. Women should not wear trousers; it is an abomination before God.

25. **GET YOUR OWN SPOUSE:** Paul advised that everyone should get his or her own spouse.

"Nevertheless, to avoid fornication Let every man have his own wife Let every woman have her own husband" 1 Corinthians 7:2-5

Get your own wife or husband and be faithful to each other. Do not allow curiosity, lack of self-control, indiscipline and carelessness to get an upper hand in your life. Stick to your spouse and send Satan out of your marriage.

26. **NUTURE YOUR MARRIAGE WITH LOVE:** The love that brought two of you together in the first place should not be allowed to die. Water it, take care of it so that it will not die but will rather grow so big that there will be no room left for the strange man or strange woman in your marriage.

27. **AVOID BEING SEPARATED FROM YOUR SPOUSE:** Always stick together. Togetherness with your spouse scars strange men and strange women away. If one is transferred to

a new location, the other should prepare immediately to go with him/her.

28. **ALWAYS ALLOW THE HOLY SPIRIT TO LEAD YOU:** As a child of God, you should allow the Holy Spirit to lead in everything you are doing. If you do, He will never lead you into sin.

CHAPTER SEVEN

$\backsim$

Run For Your Dear Life

T he twenty -eight points listed in last chapter are ways of escape from the bondage of immorality. Immorality is a bus going to hell fire. Any one in it will enter hell if the person does not jump out on time.

Delay is dangerous. Obey the word of God and do His will so that you will not cry "had I known "at last.

Hell is a place of torment and suffering forever and ever. You will not be able to manage it. Therefore, repent of your sins, confess them, forsake them and receive Jesus Christ in your life, and serve Him and do His will. Be a child of God and live a holy life. Offer yourself to Him, be devoted and dedicated unto Him so that when you die you will go to heaven and be with the Lord forever and ever. Go on your knees now and ask Jesus to come into your life.

Romans 12:1-2 says.

> *"I beseech you therefore brethren by The mercies of God that ye present Your bodies as a living sacrifice, holy And acceptable unto God which is your Reasonable service. And be not conformed To this world but be ye transformed by the Renewing of your mind*

that ye May prove what is that good and Acceptable and perfect will of God "

And in Romans 13:11-14, it is written.

"And that, knowing the time, that Now it is high time to awake out of Sleep. For now is our salvation nearer Than when we believed. The night is far Spent, the day is at hand. Let us therefore

Cast off the works of darkness and let us Put on the amour of light. Let us walk honestly, As in the day, not in rioting and drunkenness, Not in strife and envying. But put ye on the Lord Jesus Christ and make not provisions for The flesh to fulfil the lusts thereof"

And in the book of Ecclesiastes 12:13 it is written

"Let us hear the conclusion of the Whole matter, fear God and keep His commandment, for this is The whole duty of man"

Our duty is as the creatures and children of God are to obey Him. God does not accept any excuse for disobeying Him so in order to avoid the eternal torment in hell, one must obey God and keep His commandments, no matter how hard or difficult the circumstances may be, it is for our own good.

Child of God be warned and run for your dear life. To be forewarned is to be forearmed. May God preserve your soul, spirit and body unto the coming of our Lord Jesus Christ.

Remain rapturable in Jesus name. Amen.

PRAYER POINTS

Pray these prayers with aggression.

- You curse of immorality operating in my life break and die in Jesus name.
- Any power, any spirit or evil personality that wants to lead me astray be paralyzed in Jesus name.
- You spirit of error my life is not your candidate die by fire in Jesus name.
- Every control and influence of queen of heaven over my life die by fire.
- Every evil arrow of queen of heaven in my life, come out and die.
- Any dog pursuing my life, die by fire.
- I jump out of the bus of immorality in Jesus name.
- I climb out of the pit of immorality in Jesus name.
- I release myself from the bondage of immorality.
- I break every yoke of immorality in Jesus name.
- You my eyes be delivered from lust in Jesus name.
- You my feet, you will not lead me into sin in Jesus name.
- Any child of Belial planning to lure me into sin fail woefully in Jesus name.
- Any power assigned to destroy my marriage, die.
- Any spirit wife/husband defiling my spirit man, die by fire.
- Power of holiness and righteousness fall upon my life.
- Fear and love of God possess my life in Jesus name.

- Knowledge of God and the word of God be my portion.
- Blood of Jesus and the water of life cleanse me in and out in Jesus name.
- Holy Spirit of God lead me on the right path.
- Empower me O God to be a doer of your word.

PRAYER POINTS

1. You curse of immorality operating in my life, break and die

2. Any power, any spirit or evil friend that wants to lead me astray, be

3. paralysed in Jesus name.

4. You spirit of error, my life is not your candidate

5. Every control and influence of queen of heaven in my life die by fire

6. Every evil arrow of queen of heaven in my life, come out and die

7. Any dog pursuing my life die by fire in Jesus name

8. I jump out of the bus of immorality in Jesus name

9. I climb out of the pit of immorality in Jesus name

10. I release myself from the bondage of immorality

11. I break every yoke of immorality in Jesus name

12. You my eyes, be delivered from lust in Jesus name

13. You my feet, you will not lead me into sin in Jesus name

14. Any child of Belial planning to seduce me, die in Jesus name

15. Any power assigned to destroy my marriage, die in Jesus name

16. Any spirit wife/spirit husband, defiling my spirit man, die in Jesus name

17. Power of holiness and righteousness, fall upon me in Jesus name

18. Fear and love of God, possess my life in Jesus name

19. Knowledge of God and the word of God shall be my portion in Jesus name

20. Blood of Jesus and the water of life, cleanse me in and out

21. Holy Spirit of God lead me in the right part in Jesus name

22. Empower me O God to be a doer of your word in Jesus name

OTHER BOOKS BY THE SAME AUTHOR

1. 50 Ugly Faces Of Immorality
2. The End Time Army Of The Lord
3. Activities Of Spirit Husbands And Spirit Wives Exposed
4. Activities Of Queen Of Heaven Exposed
5. Seven Sorrows Of Satan
6. Ministrial Pitfalls
7. Power Over The Laptrap
8. Prayer Eagle On The Mountain
9. The Ministry And The Military
10. Ministerial Eagle
11. The Secrets Of The Witchcraft Kingdom Exposed
12. Seven Simple Steps To Salvation
13. A Hole In The Wall Of Senegal
14. The Word Of God, The Power Of God
15. I Shall Not Marry My Enemy
16. Men Of Glory And Honour
17. 20 Secrets Of Great And Multiple Breakthroughs
18. Financial Deliverance Mannual
19. A Hole In The Wall Of Senegal
20. Satanic Signs And Occultic Symbols Exposed
21. Deliverance Of The Parts Of The Body
22. United Nations, The Anti-Christ And The Endtime
23. 20 Reasons Why Saul Failed

24. Your Name And Your Destiny (The Dictionary Of Names)
25. Joseph's Path To Greatness (The Palace)

If you would want any of these topics treated in your Church, contact the author on +221774019181

BIBLIOGRAPHY

1. The Holy Bible Authorised king James version

2. Chambers20th Century Dictionary by E.M. Kirk Patrick

3. When you are knocked down, by D.K. Olukoya

4. The Mysterious secrets of the dark kingdom by J.P. Timmons

www.ingramcontent.com/pod-product-compliance
Lightning Source LLC
LaVergne TN
LVHW091108080426
835510LV00008B/614